MODEL NATIONAL STANDARD

CONDITIONS

FOR PLACES OF

ENTERTAINMENT

and Associated Guidance

The Association of British Theatre Technicians
The District Surveyors Association
The Local Government Licensing Forum

To be

A4 size copies, which include a free CD-ROM, may be purchased from LDSA Publications, PO Box 266, Bromley Kent BR2 9ZN or by e-mail to ldsa@goldserve.net

A5 size copies, which include a free CD-ROM, may be purchased from ABTT, 47 Bermondsey Street, London SE1 3XT or by e-mail to office@abtt.org.uk or from Entertainment Technology Press Ltd, 1 Kiln House Yard, Baldock Street, Royston, Herts SG8 5AY or www.etnow.com

A Standing Committee, which includes members from the industry and licensing authorities, will keep the Model Conditions under review. It will consider additions, deletions and modifications in the light of experience and developments. Users who wish to comment upon the document should write to Dr Colin Manchester, at the School of Law, University of Birmingham, PO Box 363, Birmingham B15 2TT or by e-mail to C.D.Manchester@bham.ac.uk

Revisions of the Model National Standard Conditions may be issued from time to time. Purchasers can download updates from the internet.
Visit http://www.etnow.com *click on BOOKS, click on Order Titles Available Now. In the list of ABTT publications, click on Model National Standard Conditions and click on the required update shown at the bottom of the description. When asked for the password, enter "Venue17"*

First published January 2002 Revised September 2002
ISBN Number   1 904031 11 4

MODEL NATIONAL STANDARD CONDITIONS FOR PLACES OF ENTERTAINMENT

RECOMMENDED BY :
The ASSOCIATION OF BRITISH THEATRE TECHNICIANS,
The ASSOCIATION OF BUILDING ENGINEERS,
The ASSOCIATION OF LONDON GOVERNMENT,
The BRITISH ENTERTAINMENT & DISCOTHEQUE
ASSOCIATION,
The BRITISH INSTITUTE OF INNKEEPING,
The CHARTERED INSTITUTE OF ENVIRONMENTAL
HEALTH,
The DISTRICT SURVEYORS ASSOCIATION,
The LOCAL GOVERNMENT ASSOCIATION,
The LOCAL GOVERNMENT LICENSING FORUM,
The ROYAL INSTITUTE OF CHARTERED SURVEYORS,
The SOCIETY OF ENTERTAINMENT LICENSING
PRACTITIONERS and
The TRADING STANDARDS INSTITUTE

FOREWORD

A licence is generally required to permit premises to be used for:
(a)   public dancing, music or similar entertainment and certain private music and music and dancing promoted for private gain
(b)   indoor sports where the public are admitted as spectators
(c)   the public performance of plays or (within London only) performances of plays promoted for private gain
(d)   film exhibitions where the public are admitted on payment or where the exhibition is promoted for private gain.

The principal primary legislation concerned is:
Schedule 1 to the Local Government (Miscellaneous Provisions) Act 1982 (outside London)
Schedule 12 to the London Government Act 1963 (for London)
Private Places of Entertainment (Licensing) Act 1967
Theatres Act 1968
Cinemas Act 1985

Note to Licensing Authorities

Model National Standard Conditions

These *Model National Standard Conditions* cover operational matters and complement *The Technical Standards for Places of Entertainment*, which cover the physical requirements for building and maintaining entertainment premises. *The Model National Standard Conditions* are provided for the use of Councils and licensees nation-wide in the interests of achieving a more uniform approach to licensing issues. They also provide a guide to good practice for anyone concerned with the management of places of entertainment.

These *Model National Standard Conditions* for use by Councils in England and Wales when licensing places of entertainment were developed from two sources:
(1)   *The Model Rules of Management for Places of Public Entertainment* published by the District Surveyors Association and the Association of British Theatre Technicians (which had their origins in the Lord Chamberlain's Rules and the supplementary technical requirements originated by the London County Council); and
(2)   The Model National Standard Conditions for Places of Public Entertainment published by the Local Government Licensing Forum.

Schedule 12 to the London Government Act 1963 and Schedule 1 to the Local Government (Miscellaneous Provisions) Act 1982 permit licensing authorities to make regulations prescribing standard conditions applicable to all or any class of entertainment licence. In London there are similar provisions in relation to licences granted under the Private Places of Entertainment (Licensing) Act 1967, the Theatres Act 1968 and the Cinemas Act 1985.

The Model National Standard Conditions have been designed to ensure consistency throughout the country. Councils are, therefore, encouraged to adopt them as they stand. Particular care has been taken in their preparation to ensure that the Model Conditions are suitable for use with all sizes and types of entertainment premises. Councils are particularly urged to avoid the temptation to make additional Standard Conditions or to change these Model Conditions. Any additional conditions should be added as Special Conditions.

Equally, however, when considering individual licence applications Councils should consider in each case whether each Standard Condition is applicable. Where appropriate, particular Standard Conditions should be dispensed with or modified in respect of the particular application. Any waiver or modification of a Standard Condition should be indicated on the licence document.

It is also open to an applicant for a licence to ask the Council to waive or modify one or more particular Standard Conditions. The Council should carefully consider any such application.

In this connection Councils outside London should bear in mind that there is no power to make standard conditions in respect of licences granted under the Private Places of Entertainment (Licensing) Act 1967, the Theatres Act 1968 or the Cinemas Act 1985. Consequently all conditions attached to licences granted under these enactments will be Special Conditions even if referred to as Standard Conditions. Before attaching these *Model National Standard Conditions* to a licence granted under these enactments the Council will need to be satisfied that each such condition attached can be justified in respect of the particular licence.

The Model Conditions contain optional conditions relating to good order and sex-related use. It is for each Council to decide whether it wishes to include either or both of these conditions in its own standard conditions.

A number of the Standard Conditions enable the Council to grant a consent. When granting a consent the Council can impose additional appropriate conditions, which it should specify in writing and which should be imposed as Special Conditions.

If a Licensee wishes any of the terms and conditions of the licence to be varied, application must be made to the Council. In London the Council may require the application to be advertised.

HOW TO USE THIS DOCUMENT

This document is intended for the use of Councils when licensing places of entertainment and to be issued in part to Licensees as part of the Council's licence.

It contains Model National Standard Conditions and Standard Appendices applicable to all permanently licensed entertainment premises (including outdoor premises) together with Model Additional Conditions applicable to:

A: premises used for closely seated audiences

C: premises used for film exhibitions, with Appendix C1 Model Membership Rules for club cinemas showing RESTRICTED (18) films

D: premises using Door Supervisors, with Appendix D1 Specimen Door Supervisor log-book

FX: the use of special effects, with Appendix FX1 Specimen application form and check-list

GO: the keeping of good order

H: entertainment involving hypnotism, with Appendix H1 Application procedure for consent for entertainment involving hypnotism

K: performances especially for children

S: the use of scenery and properties

SE: premises used for indoor sports entertainment

SX: sex-related entertainment (striptease or similar entertainment involving nudity), with Appendix SX1 Definition of sex establishment

T: premises used for performances on a stage, with Appendix T1 Guidance note: Children in performances

Annexes

Also included as Annexes are Model Conditions for use when licensing:
Subsidiary films and videos
Exhibition of films and videos in hotels
Premises used occasionally for entertainment

The Model Conditions for occasional licences are intended for use with smaller, generally indoor events. Large-scale outdoor events such as pop concerts will need additional consideration; Councils are referred to *The Events Safety Guide,* published by the Health and Safety Executive.

In relation to outdoor entertainment in the open air outside London it should be noted that a licence for musical entertainment is only needed if the entertainment is held on private land and the licensing provisions for such entertainment have been adopted by the Council. Furthermore, even where the musical entertainment is provided on private land, a licence is not needed for entertainment held in a pleasure fair nor is it needed if the music is incidental to: (a) a garden fete, bazaar, sale of work, sporting or athletic event, exhibition or display or other function or event of a similar nature; or (b) a religious meeting or service.

Whilst this publication is the copyright of The Association of British Theatre Technicians, The District Surveyors Association and The Local Government Licensing Forum, permission is hereby given to Councils for it to be freely reproduced. For the convenience of Councils the publication includes a free CD-ROM to facilitate easy reproduction.

These are Standard Conditions and do not preclude the issue of additional Special Conditions for particular premises.

It is not intended that all parts of this publication are issued to every Licensee. The following Table indicates which parts are relevant to various common types of premises.

Standard Licences		All Licensees to receive Standard Conditions with 8 Appendices + index
Type of premises	Type of entertainment licence required	plus Additional Conditions
Cinema	Films	A; C
Club Cinema	Films	A; C; C1
Concert Hall	Music	A
Discotheque/ Night-club	Music & Dancing	D likely; FX possible
Indoor sports arena	Indoor sports	A; SE
Premises with musical entertainments	Music or Music & Dancing	D*; FX*
Theatre presenting plays, operas, dance or ballet	Plays	A; FX; S; T; K*
Children's Theatre	Plays	A; FX; K; S; T
Entertainment premises providing a variety of types of entertainment.	As activities intended	As appropriate

* as appropriate

		GO; SX at Council's discretion
		H; K if requested

Other licences		
Premises, not being a cinema showing films or videos	Films	Annex 1
Hotel showing films	Films	Annex 2
Occasional use	Occasional	Annex 3 + parts as appropriate

This page is intentionally blank

STANDARD CONDITIONS FOR PLACES OF PUBLIC ENTERTAINMENT LICENSED BY ....
COUNCIL IN FORCE FROM...

CONTENTS
STANDARD CONDITIONS that apply to all premises

together with

and an index which includes all Additional Conditions whether or not attached

**The following Additional Conditions will also be supplied
as appropriate to the use of the premises:**

Additional Conditions A:	Premises used for closely seated audiences
Additional Conditions C:	Premises used for film exhibitions, with Appendix C1: Model Membership Rules for club cinemas showing RESTRICTED (18) films, where appropriate
Additional Conditions D:	Premises using Door Supervisors with Appendix D1: Specimen Door Supervisor log-book
Additional Conditions FX:	Use of special effects with Appendix FX1: Application form and check list
Additional Condition GO:	The keeping of good order
Additional Conditions H:	Entertainment involving hypnotism with Appendix H1: Application procedure for consent for entertainment involving hypnotism
Additional Conditions K:	Performances especially for children
Additional Conditions S:	Use of scenery and properties
Additional Conditions SE:	Premises used for indoor sports entertainment
Additional Conditions SX:	Sex-related entertainment with Appendix SX1: Definition of sex establishment
Additional Conditions T:	Premises used for performances on a stage with Appendix T1: Guidance note: Children in performances

Notification periods for particular Conditions		
Condition	**Notification required**	**Period**
9 (b)	Proposed use of special effects	At least 10 days before
10	Proposed use of storage cylinders	At least 10 days before
28	Loss of water	As soon as possible
38 (a)	Temporary electrical wiring or distribution system	At least 10 days before
38 (c)	Certificate for temporary electrical wiring, etc	As soon as possible
41	Certificates	Annually
C8	Showing of unclassified films	At least 28 days before
C15 (f)	Membership rule(s) for club cinema	At least 10 days before
C15 (f)	Change of membership rule(s) of club cinema	Within 10 days after
H1.2	Application for consent for hypnotism	At least 28 days before
SE1	Use for indoor sports entertainment	At least 10 days before
T1 (b)	Change of production	At least 10 days before
T3 (e)	Safety curtain out of order	As soon as possible
T7 (b)	Proposal for pop concert	At least 28 days before
T8	Proposal to use live animal, bird or fish	At least 10 days before

Nothing in this table shall be taken to imply that the Council's consent will be granted for any activity or action that requires consent merely because the appropriate notification was made.

INTRODUCTION

1. The Council may by way of Special Conditions dispense with or modify any Condition in any particular case. The Council may also impose additional Special Conditions in any particular case.

2. Any Licensee may apply to the Council in writing for any of the terms of the licence to be varied and, within London, if the Council so requires, the application must be advertised.

3. Licensees and prospective Licensees are advised to obtain any necessary planning consents before applying for a licence or a variation of a licence.

4. Licensees are advised to study carefully all of the Conditions attached to the licence, including any Special Conditions, and especially the definitions contained in Condition 2. In order to reduce the length of this document, many Conditions rely upon the use of words precisely defined in Condition 2; such words are indicated by *italics*.

5. Licensees should be aware that possession of a licence, to which these Conditions apply, does not in any way relieve employers of the statutory duty to comply with the requirements of other legislation including the Health and Safety at Work etc Act 1974, associated regulations and especially the requirements under the Management of the Health and Safety at Work Regulations and the Fire Precautions (Workplace) Regulations to under take risk assessments. Employers should assess the risks, including the risks from fire, and take the measures necessary to avoid or control these risks. These assessments should be considered together with these Conditions by those managing health and safety at the premises.

STANDARD CONDITIONS WHICH APPLY TO ALL PREMISES

NOTE: (1) The Council has adopted Technical Regulations concerning the necessary standards for licensed premises that have to be satisfied before the issue of a licence. It is a Condition of the licence that there is continued compliance with these Regulations, which are set out in full in Appendix 1. They form the basis of the approved arrangements for the issue of the licence.

(2) The contents list, timetable, marginal headings and index are for ease of reference and do not form part of these Conditions.

(3) Notes are provided for guidance and do not form part of these Conditions.

PART I
GENERAL

Application **1** These Conditions and Definitions shall apply whenever the *premises* are in use under the terms of a licence issued by the *Council*.

Note: In order to ensure the safety of *staff* and performers, it is generally advisable to extend the operation of arrangements provided for the safety of the *public* to all times when the *premises* are occupied.

Definitions **2** In these Conditions the following words have the meanings indicated. Except where the context demands otherwise the singular includes the plural and the masculine includes the feminine. Words in *italics* throughout these Conditions denote words defined below.

Accommodation limit the maximum number of people, not being *staff* or performers, permitted by the *Council* to be within the *premises* or a designated area of the *premises* when they are in use under the terms of a licence issued by the *Council*.

Note: (1) Experience has shown that where *accommodation limits* include *staff*, *Licensees* may reduce the number of *staff* present as the *entertainment area* becomes more crowded in order to comply with the *accommodation limits* on the licence. Such reduction is undesirable. Therefore *accommodation limits* exclude *staff* and performers.
(2) In exceptional circumstances the *Council* may also limit the numbers of *staff* and performers.

Approved   permitted in advance by the *Council* in writing.

Approved arrangements   the arrangement of the *premises*, (including the layout, fittings, installations and all other things in connection therewith) as *approved* by the *Council*.

Attendant   a member of *staff* on duty to assist the *public* entering or leaving auditoria and to assist in the event of fire or other emergency.

Authorised Officer   any police or fire officer or any person authorised in writing by the *Council*.

Balcony front   the barrier at the front edge of a balcony which prevents people from falling on to the floor or tier beneath the balcony.

BS   the appropriate British Standard, which may be an equivalent harmonised European Standard. All references to British Standards are to the current edition unless a date is shown.

Certificate   a written report or reports of *inspection* and satisfactory condition completed by an appropriately qualified engineer or other *competent person* and normally submitted to the *Council* within one month of *inspection*.

Note: The *competent person*, when completing the *certificate*, may indicate the period of validity of the *certificate*, which will normally be accepted by the *Council*.

Competent person a person who has such practical and theoretical knowledge and such experience as is necessary to carry out the work and who is aware of the limits of his own ability, expertise and knowledge.

Consent permission given in advance by the *Council* in writing.

Council the licensing authority named on the licence.

Door Supervisor any person employed at or near the entrance to the *premises* to ascertain or satisfy himself as to the suitability of members of the *public* to be allowed on the *premises* or any person employed to maintain order on the *premises*.

Note: The *Council* will not normally consider the *Licensee* or *Duty Manager* to be a Door Supervisor.

Duty Fire Officer a member of *staff* who has been adequately trained in fire prevention and fire-fighting to the satisfaction of the *Council*.

Duty Manager a person appointed by the *Licensee* in writing to be in charge of the *premises*.

Durably-treated flame-retarded fabric see under *Flame-retarded fabric*

Emergency lighting see under *Lighting*

Entertainment area that part of the *premises* which is constructed and arranged for use for entertainments including any *stage* or auditorium.

Escape lighting   see under *Lighting*

Film exhibition   any exhibition of moving pictures which is produced otherwise than by the simultaneous reception and exhibition of programmes included in a programme service within the meaning of the Broadcasting Act 1990.

Flame-retarded fabric   a fabric that has been tested using the methods in *BS 5438: 1989* Tests 2A (face ignition) and 2B (bottom ignition) using a 10 second flame application time in each case. The results of tests on the fabric shall show that no part of any hole nor the lowest boundary of any flaming reached the upper or either vertical edge of the specimen and that there was no separation of any flaming debris. (This performance standard is akin to that set out in *BS 5867-2: 1980* Type B.)

Durably-treated flame-retarded fabric   a fabric that has been chemically treated to render it flame-retarded. Prior to the ignitability tests set out above the fabric is subjected to the appropriate wetting or cleansing procedure set out in *BS 5651: 1989*. After this washing or cleansing procedure, the fabric shall meet the performance standard for *flame-retarded fabric* set out above.

Inherently flame-retarded fabric   a fabric which, although not non-combustible and not subjected to any flame-retarding process or finish, meets the performance standard for *flame-retarded fabric* set out above throughout its thickness. The *BS 5651* 'durability' procedure can be omitted before testing fabrics composed entirely of thermoplastic materials such as nylon, polyester or modacrylic, to which a flame-retarding treatment has not been applied.

Indoor sports   see under *Sports entertainment*

Inherently flame-retarded fabric	see under *Flame-retarded fabric*
Inspect/inspection	to carry out a visual inspection accompanied by such other test as may be necessary, in the opinion of the *competent person* carrying out the inspection, to enable the completion of a *certificate* of (satisfactory) condition.
Licensee	the person (or body) to whom the *Council* has granted the licence or who is deemed to be the holder of the licence under the relevant statutory provision.

Lighting

Emergency lighting	lighting provided for use in the event of the failure of the *normal lighting* system. Emergency lighting includes *escape lighting*. Any reference in these Conditions to an emergency lighting battery shall be taken to apply to all batteries provided as part of the emergency lighting installation.
Escape lighting	that part of the *emergency lighting* which is provided to ensure that the escape routes are illuminated at all material times. In these Conditions any reference to *emergency lighting* shall be taken to apply likewise to any escape lighting not provided as part of an *emergency lighting* installation.
Management lighting	the combination of the *emergency lighting* and that part of the *normal lighting* which, in the absence of adequate daylight, is intended to facilitate safe movement about the *premises*.
	Note: In closely-seated auditoria this would be the usual performance mode.
Normal lighting	all permanently installed electric lighting operating from the normal supply which, in the absence of adequate

daylight, is intended for use during the whole time that the *premises* are occupied.

Note: Normal lighting does not include *emergency lighting*, purely decorative lighting and stage or performance lighting.

Local Fire Control Centre   the address and telephone number which the *Licensee* has confirmed with the Fire Authority as appropriate for the *Licensee* to use in order to make contact with the fire brigade in a non-emergency but immediate manner.

Log-book   Any log-book *required* under these Conditions shall be:

    (i)   accurate and up to date;

    (ii)   bound and consecutively numbered;

    (iii)   retained in a safe and secure place on the *premises* for a minimum of 5 years after the date of last entry or for such longer period as *required*; and

    (iv)   readily available for examination by an *Authorised Officer*.

Note: Log-books may be kept in a manual form. The *Council* will accept records in electronic form provided the *Licensee* can demonstrate adequate security and integrity of the information. Specimen Fire log-books are provided in Appendix 4.

Management lighting   see under *Lighting*

Normal lighting   see under *Lighting*

Open stage   see under *Stage*

Pop concert   an event at which live or recorded amplified music is played and which could reasonably be expected to attract an audience of such a nature as could lead to problems with crowd control, over-excitement and/or unruly behaviour.

Premises	all parts of the premises as licensed by the *Council* including the ancillary parts of the building such as offices, changing rooms, workshops, stores etc which are used in connection with the *entertainment area*.
Public	persons, other than *staff* or performers, who are on the *premises*, whether or not they are members of a club and irrespective of payment.
Required	specified by the *Council* in writing.
Scenery	includes cloths, drapes, gauzes, artificial foliage and fabric decorations.
Separated stage	see under *Stage*
Special effects	any device or effect which was not included in the original licensing risk assessment for the *premises* which, if not properly controlled, may present a hazard. Examples include the use of dry ice machines, cryogenic fogs, smoke machines, fog generators, pyrotechnics and fireworks, real flame, firearms, motor vehicles, strobe lighting and lasers.
Special risks	any entertainment which falls outside the normal use of the *premises* and which, if not properly controlled, may present a hazard. Examples include foam parties, skating to music and performances especially for children.
Sports entertainment	contests, exhibitions or displays of any sport where physical skill is the predominant factor (except dancing in any form) held indoors to which the *public* are invited as spectators.
Staff	any person, whether or not employed by the *Licensee*, concerned in the management, control or supervision of the *premises* who has been given specific responsibilities by the *Licensee* or *Duty Manager*.

Staff alerting system	a system (whether electronically operated or otherwise) for immediately alerting *staff* to take appropriate action in the event of fire or other emergency.
Stage	the specific part of an *entertainment area* on which performers perform which is distinct from the area occupied by the *public*, often elevated above level of the adjacent floor; includes, where the context permits, platform, dais or rostrum.
Open stage	a *stage* which is not separated from the auditorium by a safety curtain. An *open stage* should, however, be separated from the rest of the *premises*, other than the *stage fire risk area*, by fire-resisting construction.
Separated stage	a *stage* that is separated from the rest of the *premises*, other than the *stage fire risk area*, by fire-resisting construction and provided with a safety curtain, which affords smoke separation between the *stage* and the auditorium. The safety curtain is normally installed to close off a proscenium opening.
Stage fire risk area	the *stage* and the auditorium together with any scene dock, workshop, stage basement, staff or other room associated with the *stage*. The *stage fire risk area* is separated from the rest of the *premises* by fire-resisting construction.
Trailer	a film advertising a *film exhibition*.
Standard 3 hours of opening	The *premises* shall not open to the *public* before 9.00 a.m. On Sundays, Good Fridays and Christmas Day the *premises* shall not open before 2.00 p.m. for the performance of plays.
Standard 4 hours of closing	The *premises* shall not be kept open after 11.00 p.m. for music, music and dancing, boxing, wrestling or indoor sports or after midnight for plays and *film exhibitions*.

Note: This is the standard terminal hour, which may be varied in particular cases.

Licence   **5**   **(a)**   The relevant licence or a clear copy of it shall be prominently exhibited in a position where the *public* can easily read it. For the purpose of this Condition the licence shall be interpreted to mean the licence document containing conditions specific to the *premises*, including any *accommodation limits*.

Note: Appendix 2 illustrates an example of the licence which should be displayed; this normally consists of one or two pages.

     (b)   A copy of any Standard Conditions shall be readily available to the *Duty Manager*.

Note: This will include any Additional Conditions attached to the licence.

     (c)   The *premises* shall not be used for any purpose for which a licence is *required* unless specifically licensed for that purpose.

Note: If the *premises* are licensed for several types of entertainment but are regularly used for one type of entertainment, the *Council* should be informed of any change to a different type of entertainment.

Admission   **6**
of Authorised
Officers

Authorised Officers who carry written authorisations and proof of identity, which they will produce on request, shall be admitted immediately to all parts of the *premises* at all reasonable times.

Note: (1)   *Authorised Officers* examining *entertainment areas* whilst a performance is in progress should take care not to interrupt the performance and to respect privacy.

(2)　　The *Licensee* should ensure that reasonable assistance is given to *Authorised Officers* to enable them to discharge their functions.

PART II
ACTIVITIES FOR WHICH A SPECIFIC CONSENT OR WAIVER IS REQUIRED

Hypnotism 7　　**(a)**　The *Licensee* shall not permit any exhibition, demonstration or performance of hypnotism, mesmerism or any similar act or process which produces or is intended to produce in any person any form of induced sleep or trance in which susceptibility of the mind of that person to suggestion or direction is increased or intended to be increased. This Condition does not apply to exhibitions given under the provisions of Section 2(1A) and 5 of the Hypnotism Act 1952.

Note: Any waiver of this Condition by the *Council* will be subject to Additional Conditions H. The procedure for application to waive this Condition is set out in Appendix H1, which will be sent to the *Licensee* on request.

Entertain- 8　**(a)**　The *Licensee* shall not permit an entertainment that
ment involving　　involves *special risks* except with *consent.* Any
special risks　　*approved* performances especially for children shall comply with Additional Conditions K.

　　(b)　The *Licensee* shall not permit explosives or highly flammable substances to be brought onto the *premises* except with *consent.* Any storage of explosives or highly flammable substances shall comply with Additional Condition FX10.

Entertain-ment using special effects **9** **(a)** The *Licensee* shall not permit the use of *special effects*, except with *consent*. Any *approved* use of *special effects* shall comply with Additional Conditions FX.

(b) The *Licensee* shall give the *Council* at least 10 days' notice in writing of any proposal to use *special effects*. The notice shall include, save in exceptional circumstances, exact details of the proposal including the date and time when the *special effects* can be demonstrated.

Comp-ressed gases **10** Compressed or liquefied gases shall not be used except with *consent*. At least 10 days' notice in writing shall be given to the *Council* of any proposal to bring storage cylinders into the *premises*.

Note: This Condition does not normally apply to gas cylinders used in connection with the dispensing of beverages.

PART III
PARTICULAR RESPONSIBILITIES OF THE LICENSEE

Overall responsibility of Licensee **11** **(a)** The *Licensee* shall ensure that the *premises* continue to comply with the Technical Regulations as set out in Appendix 1. No alterations shall be made to the *approved arrangements* except with *consent*.

(b) The *Licensee* shall, except with *consent*, retain control over all parts of the *premises*.

(c) Either the *Licensee* or the *Duty Manager* shall be in charge of and within the *premises* whenever the *public* are present. However the *Licensee* remains responsible for the observance of all licensing conditions.

Duty Manager	**12**	The *Licensee* may authorise in writing a *Duty Manager*, who shall be at least 18 years old, to deputise for him. This written authorisation shall be kept on the *premises* and be readily available for examination by any *Authorised Officer*. The *Licensee* must be satisfied that anyone appointed as a *Duty Manager* understands the need to comply with the Conditions of the licence and is competent to perform the function of *Duty Manager*.

Note: (1) Hereafter in these Conditions the term *Licensee/Duty Manager* will mean the *Licensee* or the *Duty Manager* as appropriate.

(2) The *Licensee* may appoint a hirer of the *premises* to be *Duty Manager* if appropriate.

Quali- fications of Licensee and Duty Manager	**13**	The *Licensee* (if an individual) and any *Duty Manager* shall:

(i)   have undertaken an *approved* training course leading to the possession of the BIIAB Level 2 National Certificate for Entertainment Licensees; or

(ii) possess an equivalent qualification, for example for concert halls, the National Vocational Qualification in Cultural Venue Administration (Level 3); or

(iii) be able to demonstrate to the satisfaction of the *Council* that he possesses all relevant knowledge and experience.

Note: (1)   This Condition does not apply to theatres or cinemas.

(2)   This Condition does not apply to the *Duty Managers* of village halls or similar *premises*, or to other *premises* where the *Council* considers the requirement to be unnecessary.

Staff	**14**	**(a)**	The *Licensee/Duty Manager* shall ensure that he has sufficient trained *staff* on duty to ensure the safe evacuation of the *premises* in the event of emergency. Such *staff* shall have been specifically instructed on their

duties in the event of an emergency by the *Licensee* or by a person nominated by him. The instruction given to *staff* shall include training on the safe and efficient running of the *premises* and the safe evacuation of the *premises*.

Note: It is important that the evacuation procedures are fully understood by all *staff*, especially where a two-stage fire alarm warning system is operated during performances.

(b) A nominated member of *staff* in addition to the *Duty Manager* shall have responsibility for fire prevention measures and for ensuring that all escape routes including exit doors are fully available.

Note: This person should be the *Duty Fire Officer* where one is employed.

(c) No *Door Supervisor* shall be employed at *premises* outside London except with *consent*. Any employment shall be in accordance with Additional Conditions D.

(d) *Staff* with specific responsibilities in the event of fire or other emergency, together with deputies, shall receive training and written instruction appropriate to their role as set out in Appendix 3. The *Licensee/Duty Manager* shall, once he is satisfied as to the competence of each member of *staff*, record this in the Fire *log-book*.

Fire log-book **15** **(a)** The *Licensee* shall cause a Fire *log-book* to be kept which shall comply with Appendix 4.

Note: *Licensee*s are advised that it is good practice to keep a general incident *log-book* in which are recorded details of each day's events. This may be combined with the Fire *log-book*. Appendix 4 includes an example of this approach.

(b) Any *Authorised Officer* shall be entitled to obtain a photocopy of any page(s) of any *log-book*.

Staff register	**16**	The *Licensee/Duty Manager* shall maintain a register indicating the numbers of *staff*, including any *Door Supervisors* and all performers, who are present when the *public* are present. This register shall be produced immediately on the request of an *Authorised Officer*. This Condition does not apply to any *premises* that are being used for a closely seated audience.

Note: (1) A sample register is set out in Appendix 5.

(2) As *accommodation limits* exclude *staff* and performers, this register may be used by *Authorised Officers* to assist in deciding how many *staff* and performers are present in the *premises* at a given time. The register will also be used in the event of an emergency evacuation of the *premises*. It is essential, therefore, that the register is properly maintained and that it is readily available.

Dancing	**17**	Dancing shall be restricted to the areas designated by the *Council*.

Prevention of nuisance	**18**	**(a)**	The *Licensee/Duty Manager* shall ensure that no nuisance is caused by noise emanating from the *premises* or by vibration transmitted through the structure of the *premises*.
		(b)	If *required*, clearly legible notices shall be displayed at all exits requesting the *public* to respect the needs of local residents and to leave the *premises* and area quietly.

PART IV
CONDITIONS RELATING TO SAFETY INCLUDING FIRE SAFETY

Approved 19 (a) The *approved arrangements* shall be maintained
arrangements in good condition and full working order. Fire-fighting equipment, the fire alarm warning system and any smoke ventilators shall be maintained in accordance with Appendix 6.

(b) No alterations (including temporary alterations) shall be made except with *consent*.

Minimising 20 The *Licensee* shall ensure that all performances or
danger activities minimise any danger to the *public*.

Disabled 21 The *Licensee/Duty Manager* shall ensure that, when-
people ever disabled people are present, adequate arrangements are made to enable their safe evacuation in the event of an emergency and that they are made aware of these arrangements.
Note: *Licensee*s are advised to obtain details of and seek to address any special needs when approached by organisers of parties of disabled people.

Safety 22 The *Licensee/Duty Manager* shall ensure that all
checks necessary safety checks have been carried out before the admission of the *public*. Details of the checks shall be entered in the Fire *log-book*; this may be by use of a separate check list.
Note: A specimen check list is provided in Appendix 7.

Escape 23 (a) All escape routes and exits including external
routes exits shall be maintained unobstructed, in good order with non-slippery and even surfaces, free of trip hazards and clearly identified in accordance with the *approved arrangements*.

Note: In restaurants and other *premises* where chairs and tables are provided care should be taken that clear gangways are maintained.

(b) All exit doors shall be available and easily openable without the use of a key, card, code or similar means. Only *approved* fastenings shall be used.

Note: Doors that are not in regular use should be opened in order to ensure they function satisfactorily.

(c) Any removable security fastenings shall be removed from the doors prior to opening the *premises* to the *public*. All such fastenings shall be kept in the *approved* position(s).

(d) If *required*, exit doors shall be secured in the fully open position when the *public* are present.

(e) All fire doors shall be maintained effectively self-closing and shall not be held open other than by *approved* devices.

(f) Fire-resisting doors to ducts, service shafts and cupboards shall be kept locked shut.

(g) The edges of the treads of steps and stairways shall be maintained so as to be conspicuous.

Curtains, 24 hangings, decorations, upholstery

(a) Hangings, curtains, and temporary decorations shall be maintained *flame-retarded*.

(b) Any upholstered seating shall continue to meet the pass criteria for smouldering ignition source 0, flaming ignition source 1 and crib ignition source 5 when tested in accordance with section 5 of *BS 5852:1990.*

Scenery		**(c)**	Any *scenery* shall be maintained *flame-retarded* in accordance with Additional Conditions S.
		(e)	Temporary decorations shall not be provided except with *consent*. When seeking *consent* for temporary decorations the *Licensee* shall advise the *Council* of the period for which it is desired to retain them.
		(f)	Curtains, hangings and temporary decorations shall be arranged so as not to obstruct exits, fire safety signs or fire-fighting equipment.

Accom- **25** The *Licensee/Duty Manager* shall ensure that the
modation *accommodation limit(s)* specified on the licence are not
limits exceeded and shall be aware of the number of the *public* on the *premises*. This information shall be provided to any *Authorised Officer* immediately on request.
Note: Where there is an unusually large number of performers the *Council* should be consulted.

Fire **26** Notices detailing the actions to be taken in the event of
notices fire or other emergencies, including how the fire brigade can be summoned, shall be prominently displayed and shall be protected from damage or deterioration.

Outbreaks **27** The fire brigade shall be called at once to any outbreak
of fire or suspected outbreak of fire, however slight, and the details recorded in the Fire *log-book*.

Loss of **28** The *Licensee/Duty Manager* shall have readily
water available the telephone number of the *local Fire Control Centre*. The *Licensee/Duty Manager* shall notify the *local Fire Control Centre* as soon as possible if he is aware that the water supply to any

hydrant, hose reel, sprinkler, drencher or other fire extinguishing installation is cut off or restricted.

Refuse   **29**   Refuse receptacles shall be emptied regularly.

Access for   **30**   Access for emergency vehicles shall be kept clear and
emergency   free from obstruction.
vehicles

First aid   **31**   **(a)**   The *Licensee/Duty Manager* shall ensure that an adequate and appropriate supply of first aid equipment and materials is available on the *premises*.

                                (b)   If *required*, at least one suitably trained first-aider shall be on duty when the *public* are present. If more than one suitably trained first-aider is present, each person's responsibilities shall be clearly identified.

PART V
SANITARY ARRANGEMENTS, HEATING, LIGHTING AND VENTILATION

Toilet   **32**   **(a)**   Toilet accommodation shall be provided free of charge
accommodation   and be kept clean and in proper working order.

                                (b)   An adequate supply of hot and cold (or warm) water, toilet paper in holders or dispensers, soap and suitable hand and face drying facilities shall be provided in toilet accommodation.

Drinking   **33**   Where free drinking water is provided for the *public*,
water   it shall, except with *consent*, only be provided in a supervised area.

Heating 34   **(a)**   Heating apparatus shall be maintained in a safe and
and cooking   functioning condition.

     (b)   Portable heating or cooking appliances shall not be used except with *consent*.

Charge of 35   If *required*, a *competent person* shall be in charge of
electrical installation   the electrical or other installation.

Manage- 36   **(a)**   In the absence of adequate daylight the *management*
ment   *lighting* in any area accessible to the *public* shall be
lighting   fully in operation whilst the *public* are present.

     (b)   Except as permitted under (d) below there shall be adequate illumination to enable people to see their way out of the *premises*.

     (c)   Fire safety signs shall be adequately illuminated except as permitted under (d) below.

     (d)   If essential to the entertainment and subject to *consent*, the *management lighting* in the *entertainment area* may be reduced or extinguished provided:

       (i)   the lighting be controlled from a position with a clear view of the *entertainment area*; and

       (ii)   an operator remain by the controls whilst the lighting is reduced or extinguished; and

       (iii) the operator restore the *management lighting* at once in the event of any emergency; and

       (iv) the escape route signs remain adequately illuminated.

Note: *Licensees* are advised to limit any periods during which lighting levels are reduced to the minimum possible consistent with the needs of the entertainment.

Emergency 37   **(a)**   The *emergency lighting* installation shall not be
lighting   altered in any way except with *consent*.

(b) The *emergency lighting* battery shall be fully charged before the admission of the *public*.

(c) In the event of failure of the *normal lighting*:
  (i) if the *emergency lighting* battery has a one hour capacity the *public* shall leave the *premises* within 20 minutes unless within that time the *normal lighting* has been restored and the battery is being re-charged; or
  (ii) if the *emergency lighting* battery has a 3 hour capacity the *public* shall leave the *premises* within one hour unless within that time the *normal lighting* has been restored and the battery is being re-charged.

(d) The *public* shall not be re-admitted to the *premises* until the *normal lighting* has been fully restored and the battery fully recharged except
  (i) where the *emergency lighting* battery has a one hour capacity and if the failure of the *normal lighting* was fully rectified within 20 minutes of failure and the battery is being re-charged; or
  (ii) where the *emergency lighting* battery has a 3 hour capacity and if the failure of the *normal lighting* was fully rectified within one hour of failure and the battery is being re-charged.

Temporary 38 electrical installations

(a) Temporary electrical wiring and distribution systems shall not be provided without notification being given to the *Council* at least 10 days before the commencement of the work.

Note: This Condition does not normally apply to electrical equipment on a *stage* provided with permanently installed distribution facilities.

(b) Temporary electrical wiring and distribution systems shall comply with recommendations of *BS 7671* or where applicable *BS 7909.*

(c) Temporary electrical wiring and distribution systems shall be *inspected* and certified by a *competent person* before they are put into use. A copy of the *certificate* shall be sent to the *Council* as soon as possible.

(d) Temporary electrical wiring and distribution systems shall be provided only for a period of up to 3 months. This period may be extended subject to a satisfactory electrical test and *inspection* report being submitted to the *Council* at the end of each 3 month period.

Note: The *Council* will normally require temporary electrical wiring and distribution systems to be removed at the end of the 3 month period or to be made permanent during that period.

Ventilation 39 **(a)** The *premises* shall be effectively ventilated.

(b) Where the ventilation system is designed to maintain a positive air pressure within part of the *premises*, that pressure shall be maintained whenever the *public* are present in that part of the *premises*.

Note: This Condition applies mainly to closely seated auditoria.

Cleansing 40
ventilation
ducting and
filters

(a) Ventilation ducting and other shafts shall be kept clean.

(b) Any air filters shall be periodically cleaned or replaced so as to maintain a satisfactory air supply.

(c) All interior surfaces of extract ventilation ducting serving kitchens and serveries shall be thoroughly cleaned as frequently as necessary to prevent the accumulation of grease and fat and at least once per year.

(d) Grease filters in extract ventilation hoods in kitchens and serveries shall be cleaned weekly or at other intervals as *required*.

Certificates 41 *Certificates* shall be submitted to the *Council* as specified in Appendix 8.

APPENDIX 1
See Condition 11

TECHNICAL REGULATIONS

Waiver	1	The *Council* may modify, waive or dispense with any of the following Regulations provided, in the opinion of the *Council*, the completed *premises* meet the intended function of the Regulations.
Site	2	The *premises* shall have a sufficient frontage to a road or to an open space having sufficient access to a road to ensure the rapid dispersal of people from the *premises* in emergency.
Emergency access	3	Adequate arrangements shall be provided for access for the fire brigade for fire fighting.
Accommodation limit	4	The maximum number of people permitted within the *premises* shall be determined by the *Council*.
Control of numbers	5	The *premises* shall be provided with adequate facilities to monitor and control the number of people present.
Disabled people	6	Suitable provisions shall be made to enable disabled people to use the *premises* including the provision of adequate access and means of escape.
Noise nuisance	7	The *premises* shall be arranged to minimise the risk of noise nuisance to nearby properties.
Means of escape	8	There shall be adequate means of escape from all parts of the *premises*.
Structural collapse	9	The *premises* and the fitments therein shall be constructed and maintained so as to minimise any risk of structural failure or collapse.

Guarding	10	Adequate barriers or guarding shall be provided through out the *premises* to minimise so far as practicable the risk of any person falling.
Fire resistance	11	The *premises* shall be adequately protected against the effects of a fire occurring within the building or in any adjacent building.
Smoke control	12	Adequate provision shall be made to control the spread of smoke through the *premises* in the event of fire.
Safety curtain	13	Where a safety curtain is provided, it shall be arranged so as to protect the audience from the effects of a fire or smoke on *stage* for sufficient time to enable the safe evacuation of the auditorium.
Lightning protection	14	Adequate protection against lightning shall be provided.
Fire control measures	15	Details of any fire control measures incorporated in the *premises* shall be provided for the fire brigade.
Electrical installation	16	The electrical installation shall be mechanically and electrically safe and suitable for the intended use of the *premises*.
Lighting	17	All parts of the *premises* shall be provided with adequate illumination. All routes of escape and all parts of the *premises* to which the *public* have access shall be provided with adequate and assured illumination from two independent supplies and systems.
Ventilation	18	Adequate ventilation shall be provided to all parts of the *premises* so as to maintain healthy conditions.

Heating	19	Permanent means of heating all regularly occupied parts of the *premises* shall be provided and shall be arranged so as not to cause a safety or fire hazard.
Water & drainage	20	The *premises* shall be provided with a permanent water supply and adequate drainage.
Sanitary accommodation	21	Adequate and free sanitary accommodation shall be provided, having regard to the type of entertainment to be given at the *premises*.
Cloakrooms	22	Adequate cloakrooms for patrons together with adequate changing rooms for *staff* including performers shall be provided, having regard to the operation of the *premises*.
Food hygiene	23	Facilities for the preparation, cooking or sale of food shall prevent any risk of contamination of the food.
Drinking water	24	An adequate supply of free drinking water shall be provided for all *staff* including performers, together with free drinking water for patrons if *required*.
Refuse	25	Adequate provision shall be made for the safe storage and ready removal of refuse.
Fire alarm	26	A fire alarm warning system and efficient means of communication in case of emergency shall be provided throughout the *premises*.
Summoning the fire brigade	27	Efficient means shall be provided for calling the fire brigade in the event of fire.
Fire fighting equipment	28	Adequate fire fighting equipment shall be provided for the *premises*.
Generator safety	29	Where a generator is installed it shall not present any fire or electrical hazard to the rest of the *premises*.

Generator capacity	30	Where a generator is installed to provide an alternative electricity supply to emergency equipment or to *emergency lighting* it shall have sufficient capacity and be able to start operating sufficiently quickly to ensure safety in the event of the failure of the normal electricity supply.
First aid room	31	A First Aid Room shall be provided in any *premises* with an *accommodation limit* of 1000 or more people (or 1500 or more people in the case of a closely-seated auditorium.)
Communication	32	The *premises* shall have adequate facilities for communication with the *staff* and the *public*.
Safety signs	33	Adequate safety signs shall be provided throughout the *premises*.
Information signs	34	All facilities intended for use by the *public* shall be clearly indicated.
Mechanical installations	35	Any mechanical installation shall be arranged so as to minimise any risk to the safety of the *public*, performers and *staff*.
Special effects	36	Any *special effects* shall be arranged so as to minimise any risk to the *public*, performers and *staff*.
Certificates	37	Appropriate *certificates* shall be provided as evidence to the *Council* that the *premises* may be safely opened to the *public*.

Note: Advice on how these technical requirements may be met can be found in *Technical Standards for Places of Entertainment*, produced jointly by the Association of British Theatre Technicians and the District Surveyors Association.

APPENDIX 2
See Condition 5

SPECIMEN FORM OF LICENCE

Shire District Council
LICENCE NUMBER   007

WEEKDAY LICENCE FOR MUSIC AND DANCING AND ENTERTAINMENT OF A LIKE KIND

SHIRE DISTRICT COUNCIL under the provisions of Schedule 1 to the Local Government (Miscellaneous Provisions) Act 1982

hereby licenses:

BILBO BAGGINS

to use the premises: The Prancing Pony, (Public Bar & Saloon Bar), Rivendale Road, Bree

for public MUSIC AND DANCING AND ENTERTAINMENT OF A LIKE KIND.

This licence is in force up to   30 September 3001   and is granted subject to the Standard Conditions of the Council annexed hereto and to any special conditions set out below:

(i)   Notwithstanding the provisions of Standard Condition 4 the premises may be kept open from 11pm on each of the days Wednesday to Saturday to 2am on the day following.

(ii)   Whilst the premises are in use under this licence after 11pm the main entrance doors to the Saloon Bar shall be kept closed except for immediate entrance or exit.

(iii)   The number accommodated at any one time in the areas of the premises listed below shall not exceed (excluding staff):
        Public Bar: 200
        Saloon Bar : 250.

Date: 13 October 3000

Licensing and Safety Team
Shire District Council
Rivendale Town Hall,
Rohan Road,
Rivendale   Head of Licensing

This page is intentionally blank

APPENDIX 3
See Condition 14

STAFF TRAINING

1   Initial training of all *staff* shall include instruction in the action to be taken in the event of an emergency and in basic fire prevention including the rules concerning smoking. The training shall be repeated at least once every 6 months.

2   Instruction and training shall include:
  (i)   the action to be taken on discovering a fire;
  (ii)   the action to be taken on hearing an alarm alert or alarm evacuation signal;
  (iii)   how to raise an alarm;
  (iv)   how to call the fire brigade;
  (v)   knowledge of escape routes;
  (vi)   appreciation of the importance of fire doors;
  (vii)   the location of the assembly point(s) in case of evacuation.

3   *Staff* with specific responsibilities for fire-fighting shall receive instruction and practical training in the location and use of the fire-fighting equipment.

4   The duties of *staff* with specific responsibilities in the case of fire and other emergencies shall be reviewed from time to time as changes in *staff* or other circumstances occur.

5   A fire drill and instruction on emergency procedure shall be held at least once a month or as agreed with the *Council*, under the direction of the *Duty Fire Officer* or the *Duty Manager*.

Note: The *Council* may *consent* to the variation of frequency of fire drills where the *premises* are used infrequently and this will not endanger safety. However fire drills should be carried out at least every 6 months for permanent *staff* or when the arrangements at the *premises* have been altered, for example after a change of seating layout or a change of production.

6   Details of training sessions and fire drills shall be entered in the Fire *log-book*.

Note: *Licensees* should consider whether it is necessary to employ specially trained first-aiders to administer first aid to the *public*.

APPENDIX 4
See Condition 15

FIRE LOG-BOOK

1		Full details of the following shall be recorded in the Fire *log-book*:
Initial training	(a)	*Staff* training in respect of fire precautions and fire evacuation procedures.
Prior to admission of public	(b)	The *inspection* of all escape routes, all exits and *emergency lighting* prior to the use of the *premises* on any day for any entertainment.
Weekly	(c)	The weekly testing of the fire alarm warning system and the weekly check of fire-fighting equipment.
Monthly	(d)	The monthly fire drills.
Three monthly	(e)	The testing of any smoke ventilators.
Six monthly	(f)	Refresher *staff* training.
Annual	(g)	The maintenance and *inspection* of all fire-fighting equipment and the fire alarm warning system.
Emergencies	(h)	Any outbreak of fire or calling of the fire brigade.
2		All entries shall include the name and position of the person making the entry.

3   The *Licensee* shall check and confirm the Fire *log-book* weekly.

Note: (1.)   The Fire *log-book* may form part of the general incident *log-book* for the *premises*

(2.)   The *Council* may *consent* to the variation of frequency of fire drills and other checks where the *premises* are used infrequently and this will not endanger safety. However fire drills should be carried out at least every 6 months for permanent *staff* or when the arrangements at the *premises* have been altered, for example after a change of seating layout or a change of production

(3.)   Specimen Fire *log-book*s are shown overleaf

SPECIMEN FIRE LOG-BOOK
This example assumes a day a page approach

Date	Details	Name and position of person making the entry
Initial staff training: give names of staff and training given		
Pre-performance inspection of escape routes, exits and emergency lighting		
Weekly testing of fire alarm warning system		
Weekly check of fire-fighting equipment		
Monthly fire drills: give names of staff and person holding the drill		
Three monthly test of smoke ventilators		
Refresher staff training: give names of staff and training given		
Maintenance and annual inspection of fire-fighting equipment		
Maintenance and annual inspection of fire alarm warning system		

Continued overleaf...

Outbreak of fire or calling of fire brigade		
Time outbreak noticed, time fire brigade called and name of person contacting fire brigade		
	Licensee's confirmation of entry	

Note: In larger *premises* a different form of Fire *log-book* may be appropriate (which may be combined with the general incident *log-book* for the *premises*) provided all the *required* information is included.

An example of this approach is shown overleaf.

SPECIMEN FIRE LOG-BOOK

> **NOTE:** This example gives an indication of the type of information that should be recorded in the Fire *log-book*. The events detailed are unlikely all to occur on any one day. Different *premises* will have different procedures. This type of Fire *log-book* may be kept in a bound A4-size diary.

Littletown Theatre
Fire Log-Book   **Page 936**

Thursday 1 April 2020
Performances of LITTLE EUSTACE and HAMLET
Fred Smith Duty Fire Officer
Mr Jones Duty Manager

9.00	*Opened premises; checked no obvious causes for concern.*
9.30	*Fire alarm test call to central exchange – all OK.*
10.00 to 12.00	*Inspected all escape routes, checked all doors to be free hanging and self-closing where required.* *Replaced one defective door closer.* *Visual check on all fire extinguishers.* *All emergency lights working.* *Haystack ventilator tested.*
12.00	*Lunch break – Mrs Biggs left in charge of premises.*
12.30	*Firecheck serviced fire hose reel on stage.*
13.00	*Returned to duty.*
13. 30	*Accompanied fire crew from local fire station on familiarisation visit.*
14.30	*Accompanied Duty Manager on check of premises, as per check-list. Removed chains from auditorium doors. Gave clearance to open house.*
15.00	*Performance of LITTLE EUSTACE*

| 15.30 | On stage to witness lighting of candle and putting out of candle. All ok. |

17.00   Inspected premises at end of performance. All clear except one water extinguisher vandalised.

17.15   Witnessed test of flaming torches.

17.30   Recharged one water extinguisher. Note nearly out of cartridges.

18.00   Tea break. Mr Jones left in charge.

19.00   Returned to duty. Accompanied Duty Manager on check of premises as per check-list.

19.15   Induction and fire training for new attendant with Mr Jones. Isabelle Walters. Confirmed Marcus Jones, Duty Manager

19.25   Staff fire drill. Confirmed Marcus Jones, Duty Manager

19.35   Removed chains from auditorium doors. Gave clearance to open house.

19.45   Performance of HAMLET

20.15   Called to small fire in FOH men's toilet. Called fire brigade. Extinguished fire and agreed with Mr Jones no need to evacuate premises. Waited on fire brigade. Left all ok.

20.45   On stage to witness lighting of flaming torches and putting out. All ok.

22.45   Inspected premises at end of performance. All clear.

23.30   Locked up.

         Signed: Fred Smith, Duty Fire Officer

00.15   Called back to theatre – reported smell of gas. Turned off gas main and called Gas Board to attend 08.00 Friday.

         Confirmed Marcus Jones, Duty Manager

APPENDIX 5
See Condition 16

SPECIMEN STAFF DUTY REGISTER

PREMISES:

DATE	NAME	TIME IN	TIME OUT
	* Duty Manager		
	* Duty Fire Officer		
	* Duty electrician		
	* First-aider		

* NOTE: It may assist good management if key staff functions are indicated such as *Duty Manager*, *Duty Fire Officer*, First-aider where appropriate.

This page is intentionally blank

APPENDIX 6
See Condition 19

MAINTENANCE OF FIRE-FIGHTING EQUIPMENT, FIRE ALARM WARNING SYSTEMS & SMOKE VENTILATORS

FIRE-FIGHTING EQUIPMENT

1. **(a)** The *approved* fire-fighting equipment shall be kept in the *approved* positions and be maintained in satisfactory working order, unobstructed and available for immediate use.

(b) All fire-fighting equipment shall be visually checked weekly.
Note: The *Council* may *consent* to the variation of frequency of checks where the *premises* are used infrequently and this will not endanger safety.

(c) Portable fire-fighting equipment shall be *inspected* at least once a year in accordance with *BS 5306-3* and recharged where necessary in compliance with the manufacturer's instructions. The date of the *inspection* shall be clearly marked on the appliance or on a stout tab securely attached to it and recorded in the Fire *log-book*.

(d) Hose reels, drenchers and sprinklers shall be *inspected* in accordance with *BS 5306* once a year to ensure that they are in working order. The date of the *inspection* shall be clearly marked on the control valves and recorded in the Fire *log-book*.

(e) For details of the *certificates required* see Appendix 8.

FIRE ALARM WARNING SYSTEM

2. **(a)** Any fire alarm warning system shall be maintained in satisfactory working order.

(b) The system shall be tested weekly.
Note: The *Council* may *consent* to the variation of frequency of tests where the *premises* are used infrequently and this will not endanger safety.

(c) All checks, tests and *inspections* shall be recorded in the Fire *logbook*.

(d) For details of the *certificates required* see Appendix 8.

SMOKE VENTILATORS

3. **(a)** Any smoke ventilators shall be maintained in satisfactory working order.

(b) Any smoke ventilators shall be tested at least once every 3 months.

(c) For details of the *certificates required* see Appendix 8.

APPENDIX 7
See Condition 22

SPECIMEN CHECK LIST

To be used as a guide by the Duty Manager or other persons carrying out a safety check on each occasion before the public are admitted.

Date _____ Time _____

Name of person carrying out inspection _____

Job title of person carrying out inspection _____

Do not open the premises until any problems have been rectified	Tick only if everything in order
1. Exit doors are available for use.	☐
2. Chains or other removable fastenings are removed from exit doors and hung in their approved storage position.	☐
3. Panic bolts and panic latches are in working order.	☐
4. Doors, gates or shutters that should be locked open are locked in the open position.	☐
5. All internal and external escape routes and all exit doors are clear and free from obstruction.	☐
6. Fire doors are shut unless held open by fully operational approved devices.	☐
7. All escape routes including stairways and all escape route signs are adequately illuminated (by 2 sources where provided.)	☐

8. Where 2 power supplies are provided e.g. mains and battery, both are fully operative.

9. There are no obvious fire hazards such as combustible waste or litter.

10. Fire-fighting equipment is in position and available for use.

11. The required number of trained staff is present.

12. First aid equipment is available for use.

13. Any public address system is in working order.

14. Any fire alarm warning system is in working order and is set to performance mode (where applicable).

15. Any evacuation facilities for disabled people are in working order.

APPENDIX 8
See Condition 41

CERTIFICATES TO BE
SUBMITTED TO THE COUNCIL

1   *Certificates* shall be submitted to the *Council* at least once every year as detailed below.

Note: Where a *certificate* covers a period of more than one year it will be sufficient to submit a photocopy of the *certificate* each year that the *certificate* remains valid.

Battery   **(a)**   The *emergency lighting* battery (including any self-contained units) and associated control equipment. The *inspection* of the battery and control equipment shall be in accordance with *BS 5266-1*. The *certificate* shall be signed by a Corporate Member of the Institution of Electrical Engineers or a member of the Electrical Contractors Association or by a contractor enrolled with the National Inspection Council for Electrical Installation Contracting or, with *consent,* another *competent person.*

Note: (1) A *competent person* could, for example, be from a battery manufacturer.

(2) This Condition does not apply to *premises* licensed only for *film exhibitions*. At such *premises* the Cinematograph (Safety) Regulations 1955 require that any battery used to supply *escape lighting* shall be capacity tested every 6 months and the date and result of the test entered in a register which shall be available for examination by *Authorised Officers.*

(3) A *certificate* is *required* in respect of any battery installed as part of a generator installation providing emergency power to the *premises* or for other stand-by emergency power supplies.

Electrical **(b)** The entire electrical installation (including the
installation *emergency lighting* installation but excluding any
battery.) The *inspection* shall be in accordance with
Guidance Note 3 to *BS 7671*. In large or complex
premises the electrical installation shall be visually
inspected once a year and at least 20% of the
installation tested in accordance with a programme
approved by the *Council* such that the whole
installation is tested every 5 years. The *certificate* shall
be signed by a Corporate Member of the Institution
of Electrical Engineers or a member of the Electrical
Contractors Association or by a contractor currently
enrolled with the National Inspection Council for
Electrical Installation Contracting or, with *consent*,
another *competent person*.

Note: (1) This Condition does not apply to *premises* licensed
only for *film exhibitions*. At such *premises* a
certificate which accords with the Cinematograph
(Safety) Regulations 1955 will suffice.

(2) A *certificate* is *required* in respect of any generator
installation providing emergency power to the *premises*.

Boilers **(c)** Any steam boiler, any electrode boiler working on a
and calorifiers closed water system or any calorifier incorporating a
steam receiver. A boiler insurance company shall issue
the *certificate* of thorough examination and test.

Fire alarm **(d)** Confirmation from a fire alarm company or, with
warning system *consent*, another *competent person* that the fire alarm
warning system continues to satisfy the requirements of
BS 5839.

Fire-fighting **(e)** All portable fire-fighting equipment together with any
equipment hose reels or sprinklers in accordance with *BS 5306*.

Mechanical installations	**(f)**	**(i)**	Any passenger lifts or escalators.

(ii) All lifting equipment and any permanently suspended equipment. These *certificates* should be copies of the records of examination provided under the Lifting Operations and Lifting Equipment Regulations 1998 (LOLER). Any permanently suspended loads, such as permanently installed stage lighting luminaires or loudspeakers or flown cinema screens, shall be treated as forming part of the lifting equipment installation and be examined by the *competent person* making the examination.

(iii) The safety curtain, its operating gear and controls, the smoke ventilators and drencher.

(iv) Any other mechanical installation (for example, stage, orchestra or organ lifts, revolving or moving platforms) if *required*.

Note: Where a complex mechanical installation has been provided for a production the *Council* may require *certificates* to be submitted at three monthly intervals.

Lasers **(g)** Any permanently installed lasers, other than Class 1 and Class 2 lasers.

Special effects **(h)** Permanently installed smoke machines, fog generators and strobe lighting.

Ceilings **(i)** Ceilings and ornamental plasterwork, if *required*.

Gas installation **(j)** Any gas installation and any gas appliances, if *required*. A member of the Council for Registered Gas Installers (CORGI) shall complete the *certificate*.

This page is intentionally blank

INDEX

Note: This index covers the Standard Conditions, Appendices 1 – 8 and all Additional Conditions and their appendices. Most premises will not be issued with all the Additional Conditions.

This page is intentionally blank

ADDITIONAL CONDITIONS A:
APPLICABLE TO PREMISES USED FOR
CLOSELY SEATED AUDIENCES

See also Additional Conditions C for *premises* used for *film exhibitions* and
Additional Conditions T for *premises* used for performances on a *stage*

Attendants A1   **(a)**   Unless the *Council* requires or approves otherwise the number of *attendants* on each floor or tier in a closely-seated auditorium shall be as set out on the table below.

Number of members of *public* present on a floor or tier	Minimum number of *attendants required* to be present on that floor or tier
1 – 100	One
101 – 250	Two
251 – 500	Three
501 – 750	Four
751 – 1000	Five
and one additional *attendant* for each additional 250 persons (or part thereof).	

Note: The requirement for cinemas is dealt with in Additional Conditions C1 & C2.

(b)   *Attendants* shall not be engaged in any duties that would hinder the prompt discharge of their duties in the event of any emergency or entail their absence from that floor, tier, or auditorium where they are on duty.

(c)   Any *attendant* shall be readily identifiable to the *public*.

Seating   **A2**   **(a)**   The *premises* shall not be used for a closely-seated audience, except in accordance with the *approved* seating plan(s), a copy of which shall be kept available at the *premises* and shall be shown to any *Authorised Officer* on request.

    (b)   No article shall be attached to the back of any seat which would reduce the clear width of seatways or cause a tripping hazard or obstruction.

    (c)   A copy of any *certificate* relating to the design, construction and loading of any temporary seating shall be kept available at the *premises* and shall be shown to any *Authorised Officer* on request.

Standing   **A3**   **(a)**   Sitting on floors shall not be permitted except with
and sitting in   *consent.*
gangways etc

    (b)   Waiting and standing shall not be permitted except in areas designated by the *Council.*

    (c)   In no circumstances shall anyone be permitted to:
    (i)   sit in any gangway; or
    (ii)   stand or sit in front of any exit; or
    (iii)   stand or sit on any staircase including any landings.

Drinks   **A4**   Except with *consent*, no drinks shall be sold to or be consumed by a closely-seated audience except in *approved* plastic or paper containers.

Balcony   **A5**   Clothing or other objects shall not be placed over
fronts   balcony rails or upon *balcony fronts*.

ADDITIONAL CONDITIONS C:
APPLICABLE TO PREMISES
USED FOR FILM EXHIBITIONS

Attendants –   **C1**   Where the *premises* are not equipped with a *staff*
premises   *alerting system* the number of *attendants* present
without a staff   shall be as set out in the table below.
alerting system

Number of members of the *public* present on the *premises*	Minimum number of *attendants required* to be on duty
1 to 250	Two
and one additional *attendant* for each additional 250 members of the *public* present (or part thereof)	
Where there are more than 150 members of the *public* present in any auditorium or on any floor or tier	At least one *attendant* shall be present in any auditorium or on any floor or tier

Attendants –   **C2**   **(a)**   Where the *premises* are equipped with a *staff*
premises with a   *alerting system* the number of *attendants* present
staff alerting system   shall be as set out in the table below.

Number of members of the *public* present on the *premises*	Minimum number of *attendants required* to be on duty	Minimum number of other *staff* on the *premises* who are available to assist in the event of an emergency
1 to 500	Two	One
501 to 1000	Three	Two
1001 to 1500	Four	Four
1501 or more	Five plus one for every 500 (or part thereof) persons over 2000 on the *premises*	Five plus one for every 500 (or part thereof) persons over 2000 on the *premises*

(b) *Staff* shall not be considered as being available to assist in the event of an emergency if they are:
  (i)   the *Licensee* or *Duty Manager*; or
  (ii) a member of *staff* whose normal duties or responsibilities are likely significantly to affect or delay his response in an emergency situation; or
  (iii) a member of *staff* whose usual location when on duty is more than 60 metres from the location to which he is *required* to go on being alerted to an emergency situation.

(c) *Attendants* shall as far as is reasonably practicable be evenly distributed throughout all parts of the *premises* to which the *public* have access and keep under observation all parts of the *premises* to which the *public* have access.

(d) The *staff alerting system* shall be maintained in working order.

Minimum lighting C3 The level of *management lighting* in the auditorium shall be as great as possible consistent with the effective presentation of the films.

Note: The level of illumination maintained in the auditorium during the showing of films will be regarded as satisfactory if it complies with the standards specified in *BS CP 1007: Maintained Lighting for Cinemas*.

Conditions relating to the showing of films

Film categories C4 **(a)** The categories U, PG, 12A, 15 and 18 have the following meaning:

U   Universal – suitable for all.

PG   Parental Guidance. May be unsuitable for children under 8 years.

12A   May be unsuitable for children under 12 years. Children under 12 years must be accompanied by an adult.

15   Suitable only for persons of 15 years and over.

18   Suitable only for adults

RESTRICTED (18) Passed only for persons of 18 or over who are members (or their guests) of a properly constituted club.

(b) The addition of the *Council*'s name (e.g. Guildford) after the category means that the film has been passed by the *Council* for exhibition in the *Council's* area in the category shown.

Exhibition C5 No film shall be exhibited unless:

of films

    (i)   it is a current news-reel; or

    (ii)   it has been passed by the British Board of Film Classification and no notice of objection to its exhibition has been given by the *Council*; or

    (iii) the film has been passed by the *Council*.

Objection to the   **C6**
exhibition of a film

If the *Licensee* is notified by the *Council* in writing that it objects to the exhibition of a film specifying the grounds of objection, such film shall not be exhibited.

Note: Any objection is likely to be on the ground that in the opinion of the *Council*:

    (i)   the film is likely

        (a)   to encourage or incite to crime, or

        (b)   to lead to disorder, or

        (c)   to stir up hatred against any section of the *public* on grounds of colour, race or ethnic or national origin, disability, religious beliefs, sexual orientation or gender, or

        (d)   to promote violence, sexual humiliation or degradation; or

    (ii)   the effect of the film is, if taken as a whole, such as to hold up to ridicule or contempt

        (a)   people of a particular gender, sexual orientation, colour, race or ethnic or racial origin, or

        (b)   people with disabilities or particular religious beliefs unless such film is depicting an historical event or should be exhibited in the public interest; or

    (iii) the film contains a grossly indecent performance thereby outraging the standards of public decency.

RESTRICTED   **C7**

Films in the RESTRICTED (18) category shall

(18) films **consent of the Council**	only be shown with *consent*. Any application to permit such films to be shown shall be advertised in accordance with the *Council's* conditions governing applications for annual entertainment licences.
Unclassified films C8	Not less than 28 days' notice in writing shall be given to the *Council* of any proposal to exhibit any other film which has not been classified as specified in Condition C4. Such a film may only be exhibited if *consent* has been obtained and in accordance with the terms of any such *consent*.
Age restriction C9 (a)	When the programme includes a film in the 12, 15 or 18 category no person appearing to be under the age of 12, 15 or 18 as appropriate shall be admitted to any part of the programme.
(b)	When the programme includes a film in the 12A category no person appearing to be under the age of 12 shall be admitted to any part of the program unless accompanied by an adult.
(c)	This Condition shall not apply to members of *staff* of 16 or 17 years of age provided the prior written consent of the person's parent or legal guardian has first been obtained. This consent shall be available for examination by *Authorised Officers* at all reasonable times.
Film categories C10 **Council's** **discretion**	If the *Council* does not agree with the category of any film as passed by the British Board of Film Classification, it may alter the category or prohibit the showing of the film.
(a)	On notice of alteration of category being given

by the *Council* to the *Licensee*, the film shall thereafter be treated as being in the altered category and the Conditions applicable to the exhibition of films in the altered category shall be observed.

(b) On notice of prohibition of exhibition being given by the *Council* to the *Licensee*, the film shall not be exhibited.

Category notices C11 (a) Immediately before each exhibition at the *premises* of a film (other than a current news-reel) passed by the British Board of Film Classification there shall be exhibited on the screen for at least 10 seconds in such a manner as to be easily read by all persons in the auditorium a reproduction of the certificate of the Board or, as regards a *trailer*, of the statement approved by the Board indicating the category of the film.

(b) For a film passed by the *Council* notices shall be conspicuously displayed both inside and outside the *premises* so that persons entering can readily read them. The notices shall state without the addition of any other words:-

THE .... COUNCIL
(Here insert title of film) has been passed by
the (insert name of *Council* concerned) as
(here insert the definition of the category and
the category assigned)

Where a *trailer* is to be exhibited advertising a film passed by the *Council* the notice shall state:-

THE .... COUNCIL

*......... trailer advertising +...... film

(*Here insert the category of the *trailer*)

(+Here insert the category of the film)

Posters, advertisements, etc	**C12**	Every poster, advertisement, photograph, sketch, synopsis or programme relating to a film (other than a current news-reel) exhibited, or to be exhibited at the *premises*, shall indicate clearly the category of the film.
Flammable films	**C13**	No flammable films shall be upon the *premises* without *consent*.

Condition relating to television exhibitions

Entertainments unsuitable for some audiences	**C14**	**(a)**	When any television entertainment or part of such entertainment is described by the broadcasting authority in advance of the day on which it is to be broadcast as unsuitable for viewing by any particular group of persons, a notice to that effect, indicating the group of persons concerned, shall be displayed in a conspicuous position at each entrance to the *premises*.
		(b)	Unless *consent* has been obtained no such entertainment shall be given on the *premises* during the time that any child under or appearing to be under the age of 16 is therein unless the child is accompanied by any person over the age of 18 and bona fide in charge of the child.

Restricted (18) Category

Additional Conditions for club cinemas (showing films in

the RESTRICTED (18) classification)

C15 **(a)** When the programme includes a film in RESTRICTED (18) category the *Licensee* shall display in a conspicuous position at each entrance to the *premises* a clear notice stating:-

CINEMA CLUB – MEMBERS AND GUESTS ONLY. PERSONS UNDER 18 CANNOT BE ADMITTED TO THIS CINEMA FOR ANY PART OF THE PROGRAMME

(In the case of a multi-screen complex where *consent* has been granted the notice shall specify the particular part of the *premises* in which films in the RESTRICTED (18) category are being exhibited.)

(b) All registers of members and their guests shall be available for immediate examination by the *Council's* Officers during any performance, or at any other reasonable time.

(c) Tickets shall not be sold to persons other than members.

(d) No persons under 18 years of age shall be employed in any capacity at *premises* which are operating as cinema clubs.

(e) Subject to *consent*, a subscription may entitle the club member to attend other clubs under the same management.

(f) Membership rules for club cinemas shall include the matters set out in Appendix C1 and be submitted to the *Council* in writing at least 10 days before the club commences operation. Notice of any rule change shall be given to the *Council* in writing within 10 days of the change.

APPENDIX C1
MODEL MEMBERSHIP RULES FOR CLUB CINEMAS SHOWING RESTRICTED (18) FILMS

(a)   Only members and their guests shall attend exhibitions of moving pictures classified in a restricted classification.

(b)   Membership shall be open to persons of both sexes of not less than 18 years of age. Applications for membership, including both name and address, shall be in writing, signed by the applicant, and if deemed necessary such applicants shall provide satisfactory references and proof of age.

(c)   No person shall be admitted to membership until the expiration of at least 24 hours after such written application has been approved by the proprietors.

(d)   Members shall be supplied with a personal copy of the club rules before being admitted to membership and be given a copy of any rule change within 14 days of the change.

(e)   The proprietors may refuse to renew any membership.

(f)   Members shall be entitled on any day to bring not more than one guest to accompany the member, and the name of the guest shall be entered in the visitors' book and counter-signed by the member.

(g)   On entering the premises a member and his guest shall be bound by the rules of the club and by any regulations made thereunder.

(h)   Tickets shall be sold only to members on the production of a current membership card, and members shall, if required, sign an acknowledgement for the ticket or tickets issued.

(i)   Membership cards shall be personal to the member and shall not be transferable to any other person.

(j)   Tickets shall not be transferable.

(k)   No member shall introduce as a guest any persons under the age of 18 or any persons whose application for membership has been refused. The proprietors reserve the right to refuse admission to any person.

(l)   Proof of identity, or of age, or of any particulars of any guest shall be produced by any member or guest if demanded by the proprietors.

(m)   Members shall undertake to behave in a proper and orderly manner. Any member or guest acting in a manner which is offensive, or a nuisance or annoyance to others may be refused admission or expelled from the premises. A member may also be deprived of membership.

This page is intentionally blank

ADDITIONAL CONDITIONS D:

APPLICABLE TO PREMISES USING DOOR SUPERVISORS

These Conditions do not apply to cinemas or to theatres.

Condition D1 does not apply in London Boroughs that have adopted the provisions of Part V of the London Local Authorities Act 1995.

Note: The *Council* will not normally give *consent* to the employment of anyone as a *Door Supervisor* unless it has been able to check the criminal record of the person concerned. See Condition 14 (c).

Identity badge   **D1**   The *Licensee* shall ensure that all *Door Supervisors*, when on duty, display a conspicuous identity badge on the left or right breast. The badge shall show:
     (i)   the words 'Door Supervisor',
     (ii)   a photograph of the *Door Supervisor* and
     (iii)   the registration number, if any, of the *Door Supervisor*.

Log-book   **D2**   The *Licensee* shall maintain an accurate and up-to-date *log-book* in respect of all *Door Supervisors* employed on the *premises*. This shall comprise three distinct parts recording:
     (i)   the name, address, telephone number and any registration number of each *Door Supervisor* (whether employed directly by the *Licensee* or through an agency); the name, address and telephone number of the agency providing the supervisor where the supervisor is not employed directly by the *Licensee*; and
     (ii)   the name and any registration number of each *Door Supervisor*; the dates and times of commencement and finishing of work; the signature of the *Door Supervisor* in respect of both entries; and

(iii) details of any incident in which the *Door Supervisor* is involved, including any calling of the police and any police action taken.

Note: This could form part of the general incident or Fire *log-book* for the *premises*.

Note: (1) A specimen *Door Supervisor log-book* is shown in Appendix D1.

(2) *Licensees* are referred to *BS 7960 (Door supervisors/stewards – Code of practice)* for guidance.

APPENDIX D1

SPECIMEN DOOR SUPERVISOR LOG-BOOK

PART 1

Name of Door Supervisor			
Address of Door Supervisor			
Telephone mumber of Door Supervisor			
Registration number of Door Supervisor			
Name of Agency (if Door Supervisor not directly employed by the Licensee)			
Address of the Agency			
Telephone number of the Agency			

PART 2

Name of Door Supervisor			
Registration number of Door Supervisor			
Date and time of commencing work			
Signature of Door Supervisor to confirm entry			
Date and time of finishing work			
Signature of Door Supervisor to confirm entry			

PART 3

Name of Door Supervisor			
Date of incident			
Time of incident			
Details of incident			
Were the police called?			
Details of any police action taken			

Note: This part of the *Door Supervisor log-book* may be combined with the general incident *log-book* for the *premises* (on which see Appendix 4.)

ADDITIONAL CONDITIONS FX:

APPLICABLE TO THE USE OF SPECIAL EFFECTS

GENERAL CONDITIONS APPLICABLE TO ALL SPECIAL EFFECTS

FX1 (a) The *Council* may refuse *consent* or impose specific requirements for the use of any *special effect(s)*.

(b) The *Council* may require the proposed effect(s) to be demonstrated before *consent* can be given.

(c) *Special effects* shall be operated only by a responsible person who has received appropriate instruction.

(d) Where warning notices are *required* they shall be conspicuously displayed at all *public* entrances to the *premises* (or auditorium, where appropriate) so that the *public* may read them before entering.

Note: (1) Appendix FX1 provides a specimen approval form and check lists for the assistance of both inspecting officers and *Licensees*.

(2) Additional advice on the use of *special effects* may be found in *The Event Safety Guide* published by the Health and Safety Executive.

SPECIFIC CONDITIONS APPLICABLE TO PARTICULAR SPECIAL EFFECTS

DRY ICE MACHINES AND CRYOGENIC FOG

FX2 (a) The *Council* may require approval of the type of fog generator proposed and may require documentary evidence of the non-toxicity and non-flammability of the fog.

(b) The volume of fog shall be limited so that it does not seriously affect means of escape or obscure escape route signs. The penetration of fog into areas where the *public* are admitted shall be restricted as far as is possible.

(c) Warning notices shall be displayed stating that fog is used as part of the effects on the *premises*.

Note: Cryogenic (low temperature) fogs are produced using dry ice (solid carbon dioxide) or liquefied gas (generally liquid nitrogen or liquid synthetic air). The gases released by conversion from the solid or liquid form can displace the normal atmosphere, including the oxygen in the air, to become an asphyxiant (except liquid synthetic air, which includes oxygen). Good ventilation is essential to ensure that the gas disperses in order to prevent hazardous concentrations. This applies particularly to carbon dioxide from dry ice, which is heavier than air and can gather in low places. Particular care is necessary in respect of basements, under-stage areas, orchestra pits and auditorium stalls. Stores in which dry ice is kept should be well ventilated.

If there is any doubt about the safety of the carbon dioxide vapour present, oxygen levels must be measured during a test of the effect before its use in performance. Specialist advice should be sought particularly on the siting and appropriate detection levels for oxygen meters. Meters to monitor oxygen levels should be provided if there is any doubt about the gas concentrations present. Fog may cause irritation to those with respiratory sensitivity, including asthmatics. For further guidance on the use of dry ice machines see the ABTT *Code of Practice for Pyrotechnics and Smoke Effects.*

SMOKE   **FX3** **(a)**   The *Council* may require approval of the type of
MACHINES fog generator or smoke machine proposed and
& FOG may require documentary evidence of the non-
GENERATORS toxicity and non-flammability of the fog or smoke
before the effect can be used. Only smoke
machines or fog generators listed on the
Council's approved list shall be used unless
adequate technical information is provided to the
Council in sufficient time to enable it to
determine whether the type of smoke machine or
fog generator proposed is acceptable.

    (b)   Smoke machines and fog generators shall be sited
and controlled so that they do not obstruct exit
routes nor cause a hazard to surrounding
curtains or fabrics.

    (c)   The volume of smoke and/or fog shall be limited
so that it does not seriously affect means of
escape or obscure escape route signs. The
penetration of smoke and/or fog into areas where
the *public* are admitted shall be restricted as far
as is possible.

    (d)   Warning notices shall be displayed stating that
fog or smoke is used as part of the effects on the
premises.

Note: Smoke is the product of combustion and is made up of small, solid
particles. Fog is composed of liquid droplets. This difference is
important. Apart from as a by-product of the use of pyrotechnics,
smoke is rarely used as an effect, whilst fog or vapour effects are
relatively frequent. Most "smoke machines" should more properly
be known as "fog generators". Fog or smoke may cause irritation to
those with respiratory sensitivity, including asthmatics. The HSE
leaflet *Smoke and vapour effects in entertainment* provides
guidance. For further guidance on the use of smoke machines see the
ABTT *Code of Practice for Pyrotechnics and Smoke Effects*.

PYRO-   **FX4 (a)**   All pyrotechnics shall be used strictly in
TECHNICS accordance with the manufacturer's instructions.
including

Fireworks   **(b)**   Pyrotechnics shall only be fired from an *approved* key-protected control/firing box (and never directly from the mains electricity supply.) The key shall be kept in the possession of the operator responsible for firing the devices. The control firing box shall only be energised immediately before firing the pyrotechnic devices.

      (c)   The operator shall have a clear view of the pyrotechnic device and its immediate vicinity from the firing point.

Note: This may be achieved by the use of an appropriate closed circuit television system.

      (d)   The device shall not be operated if there is any risk to anyone. In the event of a mis-fire the circuit shall be switched off until after the performance.

      (e)   Maroons shall only be used in suitable bomb tanks in *approved* locations.

      (f)   When appropriate warning notices shall be displayed stating that maroons operate as part of the effects on the *premises*.

      (g)   Only sufficient pyrotechnic supplies for one performance shall be withdrawn from store. At the end of the performance any unused pyrotechnics shall be returned to store.

      (h)   Storage arrangements shall comply with Additional Condition FX 10.

Note: All pyrotechnics are potentially dangerous. Only pyrotechnics supplied specifically for *stage* use should be used as part of a *stage* presentation. Specialist manufacturers supply prepacked pyrotechnics which enable strict control of the quantities of components and the easy repetition of pyrotechnic effects. For further guidance on the use of pyrotechnics on *stage* see the ABTT *Code of Practice for Pyrotechnics and Smoke Effects*.

REAL FLAME   FX5   (a)   Real flame shall be kept clear of costumes, curtains and drapes. Real flame shall not be taken into areas occupied by the *public*.

(b)   The lighting and extinguishing of the flame shall be supervised by the *Duty Fire Officer* who shall remain where there is a clear view of the flame and easy access to it until it is extinguished.

Note: Additional fire-fighting equipment may be necessary.

(c)   Any candle holders and candelabra shall be robustly constructed, not easily overturned and where practicable fixed in position.

(d)   Hand-held flaming torches shall incorporate fail-safe devices so that if a torch is dropped the flame is automatically extinguished. Fail-safe devices shall be tested prior to each performance.

(e)   Only solid fuel or paraffin shall be used unless otherwise agreed by the *Council*. The amount of fuel in torches shall limited to the minimum necessary for the effect.

(f)   Storage arrangements for fuel shall comply with Additional Condition FX 10.

Note: The use of real flame will only be *approved* if in the opinion of the *Council* it can be used safely.

FIREARMS **FX6** **(a)** Any firearm, shotgun or ammunition shall be under the direct control of the person holding the appropriate firearms certificate. Firearms and ammunition shall not be left unattended by the responsible person.

Note: This does not preclude the use of the firearm by the performer provided it is returned immediately after use to the responsible person.

(b) All ammunition and firearms including deactivated, replica and imitation firearms shall be stored in a robust locked container in a room which shall be kept locked when not in use. The storage arrangements shall meet the requirements of the *Council* and of the police, where applicable.

(c) Firearms shall not contain any article or substance which could act as a missile.

(d) Blank ammunition shall have crimped ends.

(e) Firearms shall be removed from the store (together with the amount of ammunition necessary for the performance) immediately prior to the performance and be returned to the store as soon as possible after use. Any unused ammunition shall be returned to store. All discharged cartridges and percussion caps shall also be accounted for at the end of the performance.

(f) There shall be sufficient rehearsal to ensure that any flame and hot gases are discharged safely.

(g) Firing mechanisms and barrels shall be cleaned and checked before use.

(h) No firearm shall be pointed directly at any person or at any readily combustible material.

(i) Warning notices shall be displayed stating that gunfire occurs as part of the effects on the *premises*.

(j) Storage arrangements for ammunition shall comply with Additional Condition FX 10.

Note: Guns used on *stage* should generally either be replicas or deactivated firearms; both types may be capable of firing blanks (provided they are not readily convertible to fire live ammunition.) Firearms that have been deactivated to Home Office standard and certified by a Proof House and replica guns which are not readily convertible to fire live ammunition are not treated as firearms for legal purposes and do not at present require a licence. The same security arrangements should, however, be applied to replica guns and deactivated firearms as apply to licensed weapons.

The use of a working firearm, including a shotgun, would require the issue of a Firearms Licence or a Shotgun Certificate as appropriate by the police as well as the *consent* of the *Council*. Some firearms, notably automatic weapons and most pistols, are classified as prohibited weapons. The use of any prohibited weapon would require the consent of the Home Secretary and the attendance of a registered firearms dealer whilst such firearms are on the *premises* as well as the *consent* of the *Council*.

For further guidance on the use of firearms on *stage* see the ABTT *Code of Practice for Firearms and Ammunition*.

MOTOR FX7 (a) If the *Council consents* to the use of a
VEHICLES production line motor vehicle on *stage* the
following precautions shall be taken:

(i) The fuel tank shall be drained so as
to retain only the minimum quantity of fuel
necessary for the action.

(ii) The fuel cap shall be (preferably locked)
in place.

(iii) The fuel tank shall not be replenished when
the *public* are on the *premises*.

(iv) A drip tray shall be provided under the
engine when the vehicle is not in use.

(v) Arrangements shall be made to minimise
the hazards of exhaust fumes.

(vi) A *Duty Fire Officer* shall be present whilst
the *public* are on the *premises*.

(vii) Additional and appropriate fire-fighting
equipment shall be provided in the
proximity of the vehicle.

Note: Foam extinguishers will usually be
required.

(viii) The storage arrangements of any spare fuel
shall comply with Additional Condition
FX.10.

(b) If the *Council consents* to a special effect using
a vintage motor vehicle or specially constructed
engine the following additional precautions shall
be observed:

(ix) The quantity of flammable liquid in
the engine shall not exceed 0.3 litre and
shall be wholly taken up by a suitable
absorbent material in a detachable
container of an *approved* type.

(x) A screen of metal gauze or other suitable
means shall be provided between the
container and the inlet valve to the engine

to prevent backfiring to the container.

(xi)   The exhaust pipe shall be carried well clear of the engine.

Note: Similar conditions would apply to any other use of an internal combustion engine. Engines fuelled by liquid petroleum gas (LPG) would additionally need to fully meet the requirements of the Gas Safety (Installation and Use) Regulations, 1998, where applicable.

STROBE LIGHTING

FX8 (a)   The *Council* may require approval of the type of stroboscopic lighting units proposed.

(b)   Stroboscopic lighting units shall be mounted at high level and wherever appropriate the beams deflected off matt surfaces to reduce the glare. Strobes shall not be sited on escape routes, corridors or stairs or other changes of level.

(c)   Where stroboscopic effects are used in *public* areas, the sources shall be synchronised and locked off to operate at a fixed frequency outside the band of 4 to 50 flashes per second.

Note: The above Condition may be relaxed for purely momentary effects in theatrical productions.

(d)   Warning notices shall be displayed stating that stroboscopic lighting operates as part of the effects on the *premises*.

Note: Photosensitive people (about 1 in 10,000 of the population according to the Guidance Note published by the Health & Safety Executive (HSE) and the Health & Safety Executive/Local Authority Enforcement Liaison Committee (HELA)) are particularly sensitive to light. Tests have shown that gazing at stroboscopic lighting may induce epileptic attacks in photosensitive individuals.

For this reason stroboscopic lighting effects should operate at the lower frequencies which have been shown to be likely to affect only about 5% of the flicker sensitive population. The HSE/HELA Guidance Note *Disco lights and flicker sensitive epilepsy* contains useful additional guidance.

LASERS   **FX9** **(a)**   The installation and operation of any laser shall comply with the HSE Guide *The Radiation safety of lasers used for display purposes* [HS(G)95] and *BS EN 60825: Safety of laser products.*

(b)   Laser beams shall be at least 3 metres above the highest affected floor level at all times and arranged so that they cannot scan onto any member of the *public*, performer or *staff*. Supporting structures shall be rigid to avoid any accidental misalignment of the laser(s). Any mirrors shall be securely fixed in position.

(c)   Laser equipment, including mirrors, shall be placed out of reach of the *public*.

(d)   The alignment of the laser installation including any mirrors shall be checked on a daily basis.

Note: Lasers produce very intense light beams, which could blind, cause skin burns or even start a fire if used improperly. Even reflected beams can be dangerous. These Conditions do not apply to Class 1 or Class 2 lasers (such as are used in CD players, bar-code readers, etc.) The HSE publication *Controlling the radiation safety of laser display installations* [INDG224] gives further guidance.

STORAGE	**FX10 (a)**	The storage arrangements for any explosives or highly flammable substances shall be *approved* by the *Council*.
OF EXPLOSIVES		
& HIGHLY		
FLAMMABLE	**Note:**	Explosives and highly flammable substances include pyrotechnics, maroons, blank ammunition, petrol, flammable gases and liquids.
SUBSTANCES		

(b) The storage receptacle shall be kept locked shut at all times except when withdrawing material from store. The key shall be kept under the direct control of the person responsible for the safe storage.

Quantities

(c) Quantities shall be limited to the practicable minimum necessary for the requirements of the presentation.

Note: No more than 0.6 litres of flammable liquid nor 2.3kg gross weight of pyrotechnics will normally be allowed on the *premises* unless kept in a store licensed by the appropriate authority.

Smoking & naked flame prohibited

(d) Smoking and naked flame shall be prohibited in areas where any explosives or highly flammable substances are stored and notices or signs shall be displayed both in rooms and on containers to this effect.

(e) Storage areas and containers shall be indicated by the explosive or inflammable symbol as appropriate on the door or lid.

Firearms

(f) All ammunition and firearms including deactivated, replica and imitation firearms shall be stored in a robust locked container in a room, which shall be kept locked when not in use.

Note: The police will also require approval of the storage arrangements for any firearms and ammunition.

Pyrotechnics

(g) When not in use all pyrotechnics shall be stored in a suitable container, which may be a metal or wooden trunk, box, cupboard or drawer. All exposed metalwork, including any nails or screws, shall be non-ferrous, preferably of copper, brass or zinc, or be otherwise covered with a thick layer of non-ferrous metal, not-easily ignitable material or paint at least 1mm in thickness.

(h) The opening face of the storage receptacle shall carry the explosives symbol together with a sign reading **Danger – No smoking – No naked flame** in letters no less than 25mm high or the equivalent signs.

(i) Storage receptacles shall be resealed and replaced in the main storage receptacle and the main storage receptacle relocked.

Note: For further advice on the storage of pyrotechnics see the ABTT *Code of Practice for Pyrotechnics and Smoke Effects*.

Withdrawal from store

(j) Only the minimum amount of any explosives or highly flammable substances shall be withdrawn from store as is necessary for the particular performance.

APPENDIX FXI

SPECIMEN APPLICATION FORM
& CHECK-LIST FOR SPECIAL EFFECTS

1. APPLICATION FOR CONSENT TO USE REAL FLAME SMOKE/FOG/DRY ICE

This form is intended to be made up in duplicate pad-form for completion by the inspecting officer on the premises with one copy retained by the Licensee or his representative.

Premises ....

Address ....

Licensee ....

Name of Production ....

Details of Proposed Use ....

Dates of Proposed Use ....

DECISION

*   Consent is given for the use of REAL FLAME/SMOKE/FOG/DRY ICE as demonstrated at .... hours on .... (date) as described below subject to the Conditions overleaf marked as applicable.

*   PERMISSION IS REFUSED FOR THE USE OF REAL FLAME/ SMOKE/FOG/DRY ICE for the reason detailed below.

Description of effect/reason for refusal

....

I, undersigned, receive and accept the above decision.

....

LICENSEE/LICENSEE'S REPRESENTATIVE

....

A REPRESENTATIVE OF ....COUNCIL

* Delete as appropriate   Date ....

STANDARD CONDITIONS: REAL FLAME/SMOKE/FOG/DRY ICE

1. The effect shall remain as demonstrated.
2. The Duty Fire Officer shall supervise the lighting and extinguishing of the flame.
3. The Duty Fire Officer shall remain where there is a clear view of the flame and easy access to it until it is extinguished.
4. Additional fire-fighting equipment shall be provided as specified on this consent and shall be maintained available for use in the stage area.
5. Real flame shall be confined to the stage area and shall not be taken into areas occupied by the public.
6. Properties such as candelabra shall be robustly constructed, not be easily overturned and where practicable fixed in position.
7. Hand-held torches shall incorporate fail-safe devices so that if the torch is dropped the flame is automatically extinguished.
8. Torches shall be examined before each performance and fail-safe devices shall be tested. Any damage or deterioration shall be made good. Each examination and test is to be recorded in the Fire log-book.
9. The amount of fuel in the torch shall be the minimum necessary for its use on any one occasion.
10. Only solid fuel or paraffin as demonstrated shall be used.
11. The stock of fuel shall be kept to the minimum and stored in an approved store for flammable materials.
12. The volume of smoke and/or fog entering the auditorium shall be restricted and shall not seriously affect the means of escape or obscure the escape route signs.
13. Ventilation plant shall be running whilst the smoke/fog effects are in use.
14. Clear notices shall be displayed at the main entrance(s) or within the foyer for the public to read before entering stating, as appropriate, that dry ice, smoke or fog effects operate as part of the entertainment.

NOTE: In case of doubt consult the ABTT *Code of Practice for Pyrotechnics and Smoke Effects*.

Additional Conditions

....

....

....

SPECIMEN APPLICATION FORM
& CHECK-LIST FOR SPECIAL EFFECTS

2. APPLICATION FOR CONSENT TO USE PYROTECHNICS/ FIREARMS

This form is intended to be made up in duplicate pad-form for completion by the inspecting officer on the premises with one copy retained by the Licensee or his representative.

Premises ....

Address ....

Licensee ....

Name of Production ....

Details of Proposed Use ....

Dates of Proposed Use ....

DECISION

*   Consent is given for the use of PYROTECHNICS as demonstrated at .... hours on .... (date) as described below subject to the Conditions overleaf marked as applicable.

*   PERMISSION IS REFUSED FOR THE USE OF PYROTECHNICS for the reason detailed below

*   Consent is given for the use of FIREARMS as demonstrated at .... hours on .... (date) as described below subject to the Conditions overleaf marked as applicable.

      NOTE: This consent is not issued in lieu of a Police Licence/Certificate

*   PERMISSION IS REFUSED FOR THE USE OF FIREARMS for the reason detailed below.

Description of effect/reason for refusal
....

I, undersigned, receive and accept the above decision.
....

LICENSEE/LICENSEE'S REPRESENTATIVE
....

      A REPRESENTATIVE OF THE .... COUNCIL

* Delete as appropriate   Date ....

STANDARD CONDITIONS: FIREARMS

1. The effect shall remain as demonstrated.
2. No firearm, shotgun or ammunition shall be allowed on the premises unless under the direct control of the person holding the appropriate firearms certificate. This does not preclude the use of the firearm by the performer provided it is returned immediately after use to the responsible person.
3. When not in use all firearms and ammunition shall be stored in a robust container in a part of the premises to which the public do not have entry and shall be secured against access to all but the person holding the appropriate firearms certificate. NOTE: The police will require approval of any storage arrangements for firearms and ammunition.
4. Blank ammunition shall have crimped ends and be stored, handled and transported in accordance with the relevant Explosives Acts.
5. Only sufficient ammunition shall be withdrawn from store for use in one performance. At the end of the performance any unused ammunition shall be returned to store and all used cartridges accounted for.
6. Firearms and ammunition shall not be left unattended by the responsible person.
7. Firearms shall not be pointed directly at any person or any readily combustible material nor fired towards the public.
8. There shall be sufficient rehearsal to ensure that the action can be safely performed having due regard for the flame and hot gases discharged on firing.
9. Firing mechanisms and barrels shall be cleaned and checked before use.
10. All accidents shall be recorded in the Accident Book and investigated.
11. Clear notices shall be displayed at the main entrance(s) or within the foyer for the public to read before entering stating that gun shots operate as part of the entertainment.

NOTE: In case of doubt consult the ABTT *Code of Practice for Firearms & Ammunition.*

STANDARD CONDITIONS: PYROTECHNICS

12. The effect shall remain as demonstrated.
13. The Duty Fire Officer shall be present in the stage area on every occasion that pyrotechnics are used.
14. Pyrotechnics shall be confined to the stage area and shall not be taken into areas occupied by the public.

15. Additional fire-fighting equipment shall be provided as specified and shall be maintained available for use in the stage area.

16. Ventilation plant shall be running whilst pyrotechnics are in use.

17. When not in use all pyrotechnics shall be stored in a suitable container, which may be a metal or wooden trunk, box, cupboard or drawer. All exposed metalwork, including any nails or screws, shall be non-ferrous, preferably of copper, brass or zinc, or be otherwise covered with a thick layer of non-ferrous metal, not-easily ignitable material or paint at least 1mm in thickness.

18. The opening face of the storage receptacle shall carry the explosives symbol together with a sign reading **Danger – No smoking – No naked flame** in letters no less than 25mm high or the equivalent signs.

19. The storage receptacle shall be kept locked shut at all times except when withdrawing pyrotechnics from store. The key shall be kept under the direct control of the person responsible for the safe storage of the pyrotechnics. At the end of the performance any unused pyrotechnics shall be returned to store.

20. There shall be no source of possible ignition before withdrawing pyrotechnics from store.

21. Only sufficient pyrotechnic supplies for one performance shall be withdrawn from store. Storage receptacles shall be resealed and replaced in the main storage receptacle and the main storage receptacle relocked.

22. The firing of pyrotechnics shall be from an approved key-protected firing box and the key kept in the possession of the operator responsible for firing the devices.

23. The operator shall have a clear view of each pyrotechnic device and its immediate vicinity from the firing point. This may be by using CCTV.

24. The control firing box shall only be energised immediately before firing the pyrotechnic device(s).

25. The pyrotechnic device(s) shall not be fired if there is any danger to anyone.

26. In the event of a misfire no further attempt shall be made to fire the device and the firing circuit shall be disconnected from the device.

27. Clear notices shall be displayed at the main entrance(s) or within the foyer for the public to read before entering stating that maroons operate as part of the entertainment.

NOTE: In case of doubt consult the ABTT *Code of Practice for Pyrotechnics & Smoke Effects.*

Additional Conditions..

This page is intentionally blank

SPECIMEN APPLICATION FORM
& CHECK-LIST FOR SPECIAL EFFECTS

3. APPLICATION FOR CONSENT TO USE STROBOSCOPIC LIGHTING EFFECTS

This form is intended to be made up in duplicate pad-form for completion by the inspecting officer on the premises with one copy retained by the Licensee or his representative.

Premises ....

Address ....

Licensee ....

Name of Production ....

Details of Proposed Use ....

Dates of Proposed Use ....

DECISION

*   Consent is given for the use of STROBOSCOPIC LIGHTING EFFECTS as demonstrated at ………. hours on ……………… (date) as described below subject to the Conditions overleaf marked as applicable.

*   PERMISSION IS REFUSED FOR THE USE OF STROBOSCOPIC LIGHTING EFFECTS for the reason detailed below.

Description of effect/reason for refusal

....

I, undersigned, receive and accept the above decision.

....

LICENSEE/LICENSEE'S REPRESENTATIVE

....

A REPRESENTATIVE OF THE ………….. COUNCIL

* Delete as appropriate   Date ……..………………

STANDARD CONDITIONS: STROBES

1. The effect shall remain as demonstrated.
2. Where strobe lighting is used in public areas, the sources shall be synchronised to operate at a fixed frequency outside the band of 4 flashes to 50 flashes per second.
3. After setting the equipment the controls shall be locked off so as to prevent alteration during the entertainment.
4. Clear notices shall be displayed at the main entrance(s) or within the foyer for the public to read before entering stating that stroboscopic lighting effects operate as part of the entertainment.
5. Similar notices shall be printed in any programmes produced for the event.

Additional Conditions

....

....

....

ADDITIONAL CONDITION GO:

APPLICABLE TO THE KEEPING OF GOOD ORDER

Good order **GO1** The *Licensee* shall not permit conduct on the *premises* that is likely to cause disorder or a breach of the peace or drug misuse. In particular the *Licensee* shall ensure that none of the following shall take place:

(i)   indecent behaviour, including sexual intercourse, except as permitted by Theatres Act 1968;

(ii)   the offer of any sexual or other indecent service for reward;

(iii)   acts of violence against person or property and/ or the attempt or threat of such acts;

(iv)   unlawful possession and/or supply of drugs controlled by the Misuse of Drugs Act 1971.

Note: In connection with drug misuse *Licensees* are referred to the *Licensee's National Drug Certificate Handbook,* published by the British Institute of Innkeeping.

This page is intentionally blank

ADDITIONAL CONDITIONS H:

APPLICABLE TO ENTERTAINMENT INVOLVING HYPNOTISM

HYPNOTISM ACT 1952: REGULATION OF EXHIBITIONS, DEMONSTRATIONS OR PERFORMANCES OF HYPNOTISM

Publicity **H1** **(a)** The *Licensee* shall not permit any poster, advertisement or programme for the performance which is likely to cause *public* offence to be displayed, sold or supplied either at the *premises* or elsewhere.

(b) Every poster, advertisement or programme for the performance which is displayed, sold or supplied shall include, clearly and legibly, the following statement:
"Volunteers, who must be aged 18 or over, can refuse at any point to continue taking part in the performance."

Physical **H2** **(a)** The means of access between the auditorium and
arrangements the *stage* for participants shall be properly lit and free from obstruction.

(b) A continuous white or yellow line shall be provided on the floor of any raised *stage* at a safe distance from the edge. This line shall run parallel with the edge of the *stage* for its whole width. The hypnotist shall inform all subjects that they must not cross the line while under hypnosis, unless specifically told to do so as a part of the performance.

Treatment of audience and subjects

H3 **(a)** Before starting the performance the hypnotist shall make a statement to the audience, in a serious manner, identifying those groups of people who should not volunteer to participate in it; explaining what volunteers might be asked to perform; informing the audience of the possible risks of embarrassment or anxiety; and emphasising that subjects may cease to participate at any time they wish. The following is a suggested statement, which may be amended as necessary to suit individual styles so long as the overall message remains the same:

"I shall be looking for volunteers aged over 18 who are willing to be hypnotised and participate in the show. Anyone who comes forward should be prepared to take part in a range of entertaining hypnotic suggestions but can be assured that they will not be asked to do anything which is indecent, offensive or harmful. Volunteers need to be in normal physical and mental health and I must ask that no one volunteers who has a history of mental illness, is under the influence of alcohol or other drugs or is pregnant. A volunteer can cease participation in the show at any time."

(b) No form of coercion shall be used to persuade members of the audience to participate in the performance. In particular, the hypnotist shall not use selection techniques which seek to identify and coerce onto the *stage* the most suggestible members of the audience without their prior knowledge of what is intended. Any use of such selection techniques (for example, asking members of the audience to clasp their hands together and asking those who cannot free them again to come onto the *stage*) should only be used when the audience is fully aware of what is intended and that participation is entirely voluntary at every stage.

(c) If volunteers are to remain hypnotised during an interval in the performance, a sufficient number of suitable *attendants approved* in advance with the *Council* shall be in close attendance to these volunteers throughout the interval to ensure their safety.

(d) The hypnotist shall make arrangements to ensure that in the event of an emergency (including the incapacity of the hypnotist), all hypnotic and post hypnotic suggestions are immediately removed.

Prohibited actions H4 **(a)** The performance shall be so conducted as not to be likely to cause offence to any person in the audience or any hypnotised subject.

(b) The performance shall be so conducted as not to be likely to cause harm, anxiety or distress to any person in the audience or any hypnotised subject. In particular, the performance shall not include:

(i) any suggestion involving the age regression of a subject (that is asking the subject to revert to an earlier age in their life; this does not prohibit the hypnotist from asking subjects to act as if they were a child etc;)

(ii) any suggestion that the subject has lost something (for example, a body part) which, if it really occurred, could cause considerable distress;

(iii) any demonstration in which the subject is suspended between supports (so-called "catalepsy";)

          (iv)   the consumption of any harmful or noxious substance;

          (v)   any demonstration of the power of hypnosis to block pain (for example, pushing a needle through the skin.)

(c)   The performance shall not include giving hypnotherapy or any other form of treatment.

Consumption of food   **H5**   The hypnotist shall not ask a volunteer to consume any food or liquid unless he has first clearly established that the volunteer is not allergic to the food or liquid he is to be asked to consume.

Completion   **H6**   **(a)**   Except as provided in Additional Condition H3 (c) all hypnotised subjects shall remain in the presence of the hypnotist and in the room where the performance takes place until the hypnotic and post-hypnotic suggestions have been removed.

        (b)   All hypnotic or post-hypnotic suggestions shall be completely removed from the minds of the subjects and the audience before the performance ends. All hypnotised subjects shall have the suggestions removed, both collectively and individually, and the hypnotist shall confirm with each of them that they feel well and relaxed (the restriction on post-hypnotic suggestion does not prevent the hypnotist telling subjects that they will feel well and relaxed after the suggestions are removed.)

        (c)   The hypnotist shall remain available during any interval and for at least 30 minutes after the show to help deal with any problems which might arise.

(Such help might take the form of reassurance in the event of headaches or giddiness but this Condition does not imply that the hypnotist is an appropriate person to treat anyone who is otherwise unwell.)

Authorised access **H7** When *required* seats shall be provided, free of charge, for *Council* officers to monitor the performance(s). The seats shall be in a position where the officers:
(i) have a clear view of all parts of the *stage*; and
(ii) can judge the reactions of a large part of the audience.

H8 Where requested officers shall be given the opportunity to discuss the performance with the hypnotist and/or senior management before, after or during the interval of the performance.

H9 An *Authorised Officer* shall be given access at any time during a performance to ensure that the terms of the *consent* are being observed.

H10 *Authorised Officers* have authority to make any additional requirement in the interests of *public* safety. Such requirements shall be complied with.
Note: The *Licensee* may appeal to the *Council* against any requirement that is considered unreasonable.

This page is intentionally blank

APPENDIX H1
See Condition 7

APPLICATION PROCEDURE FOR THE WAIVER OF STANDARD CONDITION 7 SO AS TO PERMIT ENTERTAINMENT INVOLVING HYPNOTISM

1   Any application for *consent* for stage hypnotism shall be in writing and signed by the hypnotist or his authorised agent. If the *premises* are licensed for public entertainment then the *Licensee* shall make the application. A copy of the application shall be sent to the police.

2   At least 28 days' notice in writing shall be given to the *Council* to enable the application to be properly considered.

Note: This is especially important where the hypnotist has not previously performed in the *Council's* area.

3   The application shall contain the following information:

    (a)   the name (both real and stage, if different) address and telephone number of the hypnotist.

    (b)   details (including the address) of any professional organisation to whom the hypnotist belongs.

    (c)   details of where the hypnotist has recently performed (including the name, department and address of the Council which gave consent.)

    (d)   information as to where the hypnotist will be performing in the weeks prior to the performance for which application is made.

Note: Requirements (c) and (d) need not apply with the *consent* of the *Council* if the hypnotist has recently been performing in the *Council's* area.

(e) a statement as to whether, and if so giving full details thereof, the hypnotist has been previously refused, or had withdrawn, a consent by any Council or been convicted of an offence under the Hypnotism Act 1952 or of an offence involving the breach of a condition regulating or prohibiting the giving of a performance of hypnotism on any person at a place licensed for public entertainment. (Refusal of consent by another authority does not necessarily indicate that the particular hypnotist is unacceptable and will be only one factor which the *Council* will take into account.)

(f) details of the various acts which will be included in the proposed exhibition, demonstration or performance.

Note: This is not intended to restrict the hypnotist's flexibility. The list can include all the activities which might be included in a particular show.

4 Where appropriate the application shall be accompanied by the fee.

5 The following procedure will be followed:

(a) references will be obtained from councils in whose area the hypnotist has performed.

(b) comment will be obtained from the Federation of Ethical Stage Hypnotists and if the hypnotist belongs to a different professional body, from that body.

(c) a live performance will be seen by the officers and/or the members of the *Council* who will be determining the application.

(d) the hypnotist and/or his/her representative will appear to give evidence in support of the application.

Note: This procedure may be waived, for example where the hypnotist has recently performed in the area of the *Council* under the terms of a *consent* from the *Council*.

ADDITIONAL CONDITIONS K:

APPLICABLE TO PERFORMANCES ESPECIALLY FOR CHIDREN

Attendants   **K1**   When performances are specially presented for children an *attendant* shall be stationed in the area(s) occupied by the children in the vicinity of each exit provided that, on each level occupied by children, the minimum number of *attendants* on duty shall be one *attendant* per 50 children or part thereof.

Standing   **K2**   Standing shall not be allowed, except in the stalls if permitted by the *Council*.

This page is intentionally blank

ADDITIONAL CONDITIONS S: APPLICABLE TO THE USE OF SCENERY AND PROPERTIES

SCENERY **S1** **(a)** All *scenery* shall be maintained flame-retarded to the *Council's* satisfaction.

Note: Where non-durably *flame-retarded fabrics* have been *approved*, these shall be tested for flame-retardancy at intervals as *required* and be re-treated as necessary.

(b) On a *separated stage, scenery* made of the following materials may be used subject to any requirements the *Council* may impose in any particular case:

(i) materials acceptable on an *open stage*;

(ii) *flame-retarded fabrics*;

(iii) plywood, hardboard or similar boards; any boards under 6mm thick shall be treated by a process of impregnation which meets at least class 2 when tested in accordance with *BS 476-7*;

(iv) any other materials *approved* by the *Council.*

(c) On an *open stage, scenery* made of the following materials may be used subject to any requirements the *Council* may impose in any particular case:

(i) *non-combustible material*;

(ii) *inherently flame-retarded fabrics;*

(iii) *durably-treated flame-retarded fabrics*;

(iv) *fabrics* rendered and maintained *flame-retarded* to the *Council's* satisfaction by a non-durable process;

(v) timber, hardboard or plywood treated by a process of impregnation which meets class 1 when tested in accordance with *BS 476-7*;

(vi) timber framing of minimum 22mm nominal thickness;

(vii) medium-density fibreboard (MDF), plywood or chipboard not less than 18mm in thickness;

(viii) plastics material subject to special consideration by the *Council;*

(ix) any other materials *approved* by the *Council.*

(d) The use of plastics or polystyrene shall be avoided whenever possible.

(e) Decorative items, such as statues, made of expanded polystyrene shall be enclosed by a non-combustible skin of, for example, plaster and care shall be taken that this skin is maintained undamaged.

Note: Sheet materials such as hardboard or plywood laid in direct contact with a structural floor need not be treated flame-retarded.

Note: Whilst detailed calculations are unlikely to be *required*, the amount of flammable *scenery* that the *Council* will permit depends upon consideration of a number of factors including the structure of the *premises*, the fire spread control provisions, the fire-fighting arrangements and the specific risks presented by the performance; all of which will determine the *Council's* requirements in any particular case. Lower or less permanent standards of fire retardancy may be acceptable in *premises* provided with a *separated stage*, a sprinkler installation and a *Duty Fire Officer* than may be *approved* on an *open stage*.

PROPERTIES AND FURNISHINGS	**S2**	**(a)**	Curtains, drapes and new soft furnishings, shall be maintained flame-retarded. **Note:** Some flame retardancy treatments may cause dermatitis or irritation to sensitive skins.
		(b)	Any carpets and other textile floor coverings and under-lays when tested appropriately in accordance with *BS 4790* shall either not ignite or have the effects of ignition limited to a radius of 35mm on both upper and under surfaces.

Note: Similar considerations apply to the use of properties and furnishings as to the use of *scenery*. Where the action does not involve the use of naked flame or smoking lesser standards may be acceptable. As a general rule hand-held properties and antique furnishings will be *approved* without flame retardancy treatment. However the *Council* will generally apply the same standards as apply to *scenery* to large properties, large quantities of furnishings and to items especially constructed for the presentation.

This page is intentionally blank

ADDITIONAL CONDITIONS SE:

APPLICABLE TO PREMISES USED FOR INDOOR SPORTS ENTERTAINMENT

All Sports Entertainment

Notice	**SE1**	At least 10 days' notice in writing shall be given to the *Council* of any proposal to use the *premises* for any *sports entertainment*.
Seating and standing	**SE2**	The *Council* shall approve the arrangements for the *premises* including all seating and standing areas for spectators which shall minimise any risk to spectators, participants or *staff*.
Risk from equipment	**SE3**	Reasonable and practicable steps shall be taken to minimise any risk to spectators, participants or *staff* from any equipment used in the entertainment.
Medical practitioners	**SE4 (a)**	If *required*, an appropriately qualified medical practitioner(s) shall be present throughout the *sports entertainment*.
	(b)	A registered medical practitioner or a registered paramedic shall be present at any *sports entertainment* involving boxing, wrestling, judo, karate or other *sports entertainment* of a similar nature.
Dressing room accommodation	**SE5**	Dressing room accommodation and washing facilities for participants shall be provided to the satisfaction of the *Council*.

Sports Entertainment Involving a Ring

Construction of ring   **SE6**   The ring shall be sited, constructed and supported to the satisfaction of the *Council*. Any material used to form a skirt around the ring shall be flame-retarded to the satisfaction of the *Council*.

Occupation of seats   **SE7**   At wrestling or other entertainments of a similar nature members of the *public* shall not occupy any seat within 2.5m of the ring.

Water Sports

Rescue and life safety   **SE8**   *Staff* adequately trained in rescue and life safety procedures shall be stationed and remain within the vicinity of the water at all material times. The *Council* shall approve the number of such *staff*.

Note: The *Council* will normally accept the number of such *staff* as recommended in *Managing Health and Safety in Swimming Pools* issued jointly by the Health and Safety Commission and Sport England.

ADDITIONAL CONDITIONS SX:
FOR PARTICULAR CONTROL OVER STRIPTEASE
OR SIMILAR ENTERTAINMENT
INVOLVING NUDITY

Councils which wish to exercise particular control over striptease or similar entertainment involving nudity are recommended to use one of the following Conditions:

London Borough Councils which have adopted Schedule 3 to the Local Government (Miscellaneous Provisions) Act 1982 AND the amendments contained in the Greater London Council (General Powers) Act 1986 should use the following Condition:

SX1   **(a)**   The *premises* shall not be used for any purpose which, but for this licence, would require a sex establishment licence.

           Note: The definition of a sex establishment is set out in Appendix SX1.

           (b)   This Condition does not apply to any entertainment that is an integral part of a licensed performance of a play.

Note: The Conditions to be attached to any approval for the waiver of this Condition are set out below.

All other Councils should use the following Condition:

SX2   **(a)**   The *premises* shall not be used for striptease or entertainment of a like kind to dancing which involves nudity or the sexual stimulation of patrons.

           (b)   This Condition does not apply to any entertainment that is an integral part of a licensed performance of a play.

Note: The Conditions to be attached to any approval for the waiver of this Condition are set out below.

CONDITIONS TO PERMIT ENTERTAINMENT INVOLVING STRIPTEASE AND/OR NUDITY AND/OR SEXUAL STIMULATION (WAIVER OF SPECIAL CONDITIONS SX1 or SX2)

Definition   SX3   All references to striptease shall be deemed to include all forms of striptease or nudity, including the wearing of 'see through' clothing and sexual stimulation.

General   SX4   Only activities to which the *Council* has given its *consent* shall take place.

SX5   The *approved* activities shall take place only in the areas designated by the *Council* and the *approved* access to the dressing room(s) shall be maintained whilst striptease entertainment is taking place and immediately thereafter.

Note: The *Council* will not permit the striptease to be in a location where the performance can be seen from the street.

SX6   The striptease entertainment shall be given only by the performers/entertainers and the audience shall not be permitted to participate.

SX7   Whilst striptease entertainment is taking place no person under the age of 18 shall be on the *premises*. A clear notice shall be displayed at each entrance to the *premises* in a prominent position so that it can be easily read by persons entering the *premises* with the following words:
NO PERSON UNDER THE AGE OF 18 WILL BE ADMITTED

SX8   Except as permitted by Additional Condition SX10, the *Licensee* shall not encourage, or permit encouragement to be made to the audience to throw money at or other wise to give gratuities to the performers.

ADDITIONAL CONDITIONS FOR TABLESIDE DANCING

SX9 Entertainment under this *consent* may be provided solely by dancers to customers seated at table in the *approved* part of the *premises*.

SX10 There shall be no physical contact between customers and the dancers other than the transfer of money or tokens at the beginning or conclusion of the performance.

SX11 CCTV shall be installed to cover all the areas where dancing will take place.

SX12 Whilst dancing takes place not less than .....(insert *approved* number) *Door Supervisors* shall be employed in that part of the *premises* used for dancing.

APPENDIX SX1

DEFINITION OF SEX ESTABLISHMENT

Sex encounter establishment means:

(a) *premises* at which performances, which are not unlawful, are given by one or more persons present and performing, which wholly or mainly comprise the sexual stimulation of persons admitted to the *premises* (whether by verbal or any other means); or

(b) *premises* at which any services, which are not unlawful, and which do not constitute sexual activity are provided by one or more persons who are without clothes or who expose their breasts or genital, urinary or excretory organs at any time while they are providing the service; or

(c) *premises* at which entertainments, which are not unlawful, are provided by one or more persons who are without clothes or who expose their breasts or genital, urinary or excretory organs during the entertainment; or

(d) *premises* (not being a sex cinema) at which pictures are exhibited by whatever means (and whether or not to the accompaniment of music) in such circumstances that it is reasonable for the appropriate authority to decide that the principle purpose of the exhibition, other than the purpose of generating income, is to stimulate or encourage sexual activity or acts of force or restraint associated with sexual activity.

Sex cinema means:

any *premises*, vehicle, vessel or stall used to a significant degree for the exhibition of moving pictures, by whatever means produced, which:

(a) are concerned primarily with the portrayal of, or primarily deal with or relate to, or are intended to stimulate or encourage:
    (i) sexual activity; or
    (ii) acts of force or restraint which are associated with sexual activity; or

(b) are concerned primarily with the portrayal of, or primarily deal with or relate to, genital organs or urinary or excretory functions.

ADDITIONAL CONDITIONS T:
APPLICABLE TO PREMISES
USED FOR PERFORMANCES ON A STAGE

Scenery and properties   **T1**   (a)   Any *scenery* and properties shall comply with Additional Conditions S.

(b)   The *Licensee* shall give the *Council* at least 10 days' notice in writing of any change of production.

(c)   *Scenery* and properties shall only be stored in *approved* areas.

(d)   Unless otherwise *approved*, the doors to any *scenery* store shall be kept closed during performances.

(e)   Unless otherwise *approved*, any *scenery* and properties kept on a *stage* shall be restricted to the requirements of the current presentation. Any storage in the *stage fire risk area* shall be limited to the *approved* amounts.

Fire prevention   **T2**   (a)   If *required*, at least one member of *staff* shall be adequately trained in fire prevention and extinction. Such person shall act as *Duty Fire Officer* and shall not be engaged in other duties which conflict with this primary duty and shall be readily identifiable and distinguishable from other members of *staff*. Additional trained *staff* shall be provided if *required*.

Note: This Condition is likely to apply to theatres and other *premises* where the entertainment involves *special risks* or the use of *special effects*.

(b) All parts of the *premises* shall be *inspected* by a member of *staff* at the end of every separate performance in order to ensure no fire exists and to identify any risk of fire.

Safety curtain **T3** **(a)** The release points for the safety curtain, drencher
(where provided) and ventilator(s) shall be maintained unobstructed and in good working order.

(b) The safety curtain shall be tested immediately before or during each performance.

(c) Unless otherwise *approved*, the plane of descent of the safety curtain shall be kept clear and unobstructed at all times.

(d) Unless otherwise *approved*, *scenery* or properties shall not be placed on the auditorium side of the safety curtain.

(e) The *Licensee/Duty Manager* shall as soon as possible notify the *local Fire Control Centre* and the *Council* if the safety curtain is out of order.

Front curtain **T4** Where a *stage* with a proscenium arch is not equipped with a safety curtain, any curtains provided between the *stage* and the auditorium shall be heavy-weight and be made of non-combustible material or *inherently* or *durably-treated flame-retarded fabric*.

Smoking within **T5** Smoking shall be strictly prohibited within any
stage area stage area (other than as part of the action of the performance.) Signs prohibiting smoking shall be prominently displayed.

Temporary dressing rooms	**T6**	**(a)**	Temporary dressing rooms shall not be provided except with *consent*.
		(b)	Unless otherwise *approved*, quick change arrangements which affect the means of escape or fire-fighting arrangements shall not be made.
Pop concerts	**T7**	**(a)**	*Pop concerts* shall not be given except with *consent*.
		(b)	The *Licensee* shall give the *Council* at least 28 days' notice in writing of any intention to stage a *pop concert*.
		(c)	The application shall give the names of the groups or artists booked to appear (if known) together with an indication of the age and profile of the expected audience.
Animals etc	**T8**		The *Licensee* shall give the *Council* at least 10 days' notice in writing of any intention to use any live animal, bird or fish in a performance.
Children	**T9**		No child shall be permitted on any *stage,* whether or not as a performer, without *consent*.
			Note: If the *Council* permits children to perform on a *stage* the guidance in Appendix T1 should be followed as applicable.

This page is intentionally blank

APPENDIX T1

GUIDANCE NOTE
Children in Performances

Managers are recommended to pass copies of this guidance to the organisers of such events.

1.   Introduction

There are many productions each year that are one performance shows where the cast is made up almost entirely of large numbers of children. They may be taking part as individuals or as part of a drama club, stage school or school group. The age of the children ranges on average from 5 years through to 18 years.

The Children (Performances) Regulations 1968 as amended set out the requirements for children performing in a show over a period of time. However many of the Regulations are not applicable to single shows.

The children appearing for a single performance will not normally be familiar with the layout or workings of the venue.

These guidelines are designed to assist in the planning of such shows to help assure the safety and welfare of the children taking part. The guidelines are issued without prejudice to any statutory legislation or to any specific requirements of the local education authority and /or the local Council.

2.   The Venue

It is important to establish that the backstage facilities are large enough to safely accommodate the number of children taking part when starting discussions with the management of the proposed venue.

To assist the organisers with planning the event, the venue management will need to know:

- the exact number of children taking part.
- how the children are to be grouped for dressing room accommodation, including numbers, age and sex.
- that 'chill out' areas will be necessary for the children to relax with refreshment provided.

It is important that the Council is involved in the discussions at a very early stage to ensure that the production is at least agreed in principle and that any problems that could arise are identified and resolved.

3. Fire Safety

All exits should be available and any security fastenings removed from all exit doors while the children are on the premises.

All chaperones and production crew on the show must receive instruction on the fire procedures applicable to the venue prior to the arrival of the children. In addition it is strongly recommended that a copy of the fire instructions (including a location plan showing the escape routes) is provided in all dressing rooms and in any other changing areas or refreshment / 'chill out' areas.

The Duty Fire Officer or Duty Manager should carry out regular patrols of the dressing room corridors and all exit routes.

4. Scenery and Special Effects

Any scenery brought into the venue for the production should comply with the standards required by the Council.

It is recommended that special effects are not used in children's productions. The use of special effects, including smoke, dry ice, rapid pulsating or flashing lights, may trigger allergies or an adverse reaction in some cases.

If special effects are proposed full details should be submitted to the Council for separate approval.

5. Dressing Rooms

There is no specific formula for calculating the acceptable number of children that may safely occupy a dressing room but every child should have a seat and not be expected to sit on tables or to stand. All costumes etc. for the children should be kept within the dressing rooms and the corridors kept clear of all obstructions at all times.

Other suitable areas of the premises may be used as additional dressing rooms, subject to the agreement of the venue management and of the Council.

It is important that when not on stage, the children remain in their allocated area(s) to prevent localised overcrowding or obstruction of the corridors or escape routes.

Where dressing room accommodation is to be provided in another building away from the venue hosting the performance, the Council and the fire authority should be advised. This will enable them to inspect the premises to check on the suitability for the intended use and the fire safety arrangements.

6. Care of Children

Theatres, concert halls and similar premises are places of work and can have a lot of potentially dangerous equipment. Therefore it is very important that children are kept under adult supervision at all times including transfer from stage to dressing rooms and anywhere else in the premises.

It is important that the children can be accounted for at all times in case of an evacuation or emergency. To achieve this the following actions need to be taken prior to the arrival of the children at the venue:

- allocation of dressing rooms/changing areas with a list of the names of the children using each dressing room plus the names of the chaperones responsible for each dressing room/changing area.

- each chaperone to have a list of the children for whom they are responsible.

- the venue manager and management team to have copies of all the lists including any last minute alterations.

7. Chaperones

Chaperones are responsible for the welfare and safety of the children in their care. It is very important that each chaperone is a fit and proper person to carry out the requirements of the job. The use of persons who have been checked and approved for work with children either through a Council or by a recognized children's or youth organisation is strongly recommended (and may be required by the local education authority and/or the Council.)

Chaperones should be clearly identified, including their name and dressing room number.

The ratio of chaperones to groups of children must be sufficient to ensure that children remain under supervision at all times including escorting to and from the stage.

Chaperones should only be responsible for the children in one dressing room.

Additional chaperones may be required to assist with children with disabilities.

To assist the chaperones to carry out their functions effectively the following information needs to be provided prior to the arrival of the children:

• instruction on the means of escape and fire safety procedures (including code words and directions to the assembly points) operated by the venue.

• a plan of the dressing rooms/changing areas being used with the exit routes clearly indicated thereon for each chaperone.

8. Arrival of the Children
Upon arrival at the venue the children should be directed to an area where there is the space to sort the children into their groups and introduce them to their chaperones.

Each chaperone should check that the names on their list correspond with the children present in the group and any changes necessary are made and reported to the organiser to ensure that the manager's lists are up to date.

The children should be given a briefing on the importance of remaining in their groups and doing what they are told, when they are told.

9. Emergency evacuation during a performance
It is very likely that parents, guardians and relatives will be in the audience. It is important that, in the unlikely event of an emergency evacuation, all members of the audience follow the instructions of the venue staff and not attempt to go backstage to find their child, who will be evacuated from the premises and accounted for along with the other children. It is advisable to remind the audience of these arrangements either by announcement or notice.

10.   Collection of Children

Very careful consideration needs to be given to ensure that all children are accounted for and that, where they are not in school parties or similar groups, they are returned to the correct person.

A free-for-all collection at the stage door is not satisfactory.

Parents and guardians should be asked to remain in the auditorium until called to a collection point. The chaperones bring the children to the collection point where each child can be handed over and their name crossed off the chaperone's list.

The area chosen for the handover of the children must be large enough to prevent overcrowding. If the area is restricted there needs to be a management structure in place to bring groups of children forward in turn for collection.

This page is intentionally blank

ANNEX 1

STANDARD CONDITIONS FOR EXHIBITION OF SUBSIDIARY FILMS AND VIDEOS

Standard Conditions in respect of premises licensed by ....
Council for film exhibitions (including video) where such exhibitions are incidental or subsidiary to the main activity of the premises, in force from ....

These Conditions are divided into parts as follows:

ADDITIONAL CONDITIONS IN RESPECT OF FILMS EXHIBITED IN PUBLIC HOUSES

INTRODUCTION

1. The Council may by way of Special Conditions dispense with or modify any Condition in any particular case. The Council may also impose additional Special Conditions in any particular case.

2. Any Licensee may apply to the Council in writing for any of the terms of the licence to be varied and, subject to any statutory enactment, if the Council so requires, the application must be advertised.

3. In order to reduce the length of this document, many Conditions rely upon the use of words precisely defined in Condition 1; such words are indicated by *italics*.

PART I

GENERAL

Definitions   **1**   In these Conditions the following words have the meanings indicated. Except where the context demands otherwise the singular includes the plural and the masculine includes the feminine. Words in *italics* throughout these Conditions denote words defined below.

Approved *arrangements*
the arrangement of the *premises*, (including the layout, fittings, installations and all other things in connection therewith) as approved by the *Council*.

Authorised Officer
any police or fire officer or any person authorised in writing by the *Council*.

Certificate
a written report or reports of inspection and satisfactory condition completed by an appropriately qualified engineer or other competent person and normally submitted to the *Council* within one month of inspection.

Note: The competent person, when completing the *certificate*, may indicate the period of validity of the *certificate*, which will normally be accepted by the *Council*. Where a *certificate* covers a period of more than one year it will be sufficient to submit a photocopy of that *certificate*.

Consent
permission given in advance by the *Council* in writing.

Council
the licensing authority named on the licence.

Emergency lighting
lighting provided for use in the event of the failure of the *normal lighting* system. Emergency lighting

includes escape lighting. Any reference in these Conditions to an emergency lighting battery shall be taken to apply all batteries provided as part of the emergency lighting installation.

Film exhibition   any exhibition of moving pictures which is produced otherwise than by the simultaneous reception and exhibition of programmes included in a programme service within the meaning of the Broadcasting Act 1990.

Normal lighting   all permanently installed electric lighting operating from the normal supply which, in the absence of adequate daylight, is intended for use during the whole time that the *premises* are occupied.

Note: Normal lighting does not include *emergency lighting*, purely decorative lighting and stage or performance lighting.

Premises   all parts of the premises as licensed by the *Council* including the ancillary parts of the building such as offices, changing rooms, workshops, stores etc which are used in connection with the entertainment area.

Trailer   a film advertising a *film exhibition*.

Scope of licence 2   The film licence shall be restricted to:-
(a)   the exhibition of moving pictures supplementing music produced by electronic means such as a juke box; and/or

(b)   the exhibition of moving pictures as an accompaniment to the dancing (for example at discotheques); and/or

(c)   the exhibition of films in public houses.

PART II

PARTICULAR RESPONSIBILITIES OF LICENSEE

Responsibility 3 **(a)** The Licensee shall, except with *consent*, retain
of Licensee control over all parts of the *premises*.

(b) Either the Licensee or the Duty Manager shall be in charge of and within the *premises* whenever the *premises* are in use for the purposes of the licence. However the *Licensee* remains responsible for the observance of all licensing conditions.

(c) The Licensee may authorise in writing a Duty Manager, who shall be at least 18 years old, to deputise for him. This written authorisation shall be kept on the *premises* and be readily available for examination by any *Authorised Officer*. The Licensee must be satisfied that anyone appointed as a Duty Manager understands the need to comply with the Conditions of the licence and is competent to perform the function of Duty Manager.

Note: Hereafter in these Conditions the term 'Licensee' will mean the Licensee or the Duty Manager as appropriate.

Staff 4 The Licensee shall ensure that he has sufficient trained staff on duty to ensure the safe evacuation of the *premises* in the event of emergency. Such staff shall have been specifically instructed on their duties in the event of an emergency by the Licensee or by a person nominated by him. The instruction given to staff shall include training on the safe and efficient running of the *premises* and the safe evacuation of the *premises*.

PART III

CONDITIONS RELATING TO SAFETY INCLUDING FIRE SAFETY

Maintenance and testing   **5**   **(a)**   The *approved arrangements,* including the means of escape provisions, the fire alarm warning system, the fire-fighting equipment, the electrical installation and any mechanical equipment, shall be maintained in good condition and full working order.

(b)   No alterations (including temporary alterations) shall be made except with *consent.*

Escape routes   **6**   **(a)**   All escape routes and exits including external exits shall be maintained unobstructed, in good order with non-slippery and even surfaces, free of trip hazards and clearly identified in accordance with the *approved arrangements.*

Note: In *premises* where chairs and tables are provided care should be taken that clear gangways are maintained.

(b)   All exit doors shall be available and easily openable without the use of a key, card, code or similar means. Only approved fastenings shall be used.

Note: Doors that are not in regular use should be opened in order to ensure they function satisfactorily.

(c)   Any removable security fastenings shall be removed from the doors prior to opening the *premises* to the public. All such fastenings shall be kept in the approved position(s).

(d)   If required, exit doors shall be secured in the fully open position when the public are present.

(e) All fire doors shall be maintained effectively self-closing and shall not be held open other than by approved devices.

(f) Fire-resisting doors to ducts, service shafts and cupboards shall be kept locked shut.

(g) The edges of the treads of steps and stairways shall be maintained so as to be conspicuous.

Overcrowding 7 The Licensee shall ensure that the accommodation limit(s) specified on the licence are not exceeded and shall be aware of the number of the public on the *premises*. This information shall be provided to any *Authorised Officer* immediately on request.

Outbreaks of fire 8 The fire brigade shall be called at once to any outbreak or suspected outbreak of fire, however slight.

Disabled people 9 The Licensee shall ensure that, whenever disabled people are present, adequate arrangements are made to enable their safe evacuation in the event of an emergency and that they are made aware of these arrangements.

PART IV

LIGHTING AND ELECTRICAL INSTALLATIONS

Lighting 10 Two independent systems of lighting (*normal*
(normal and *lighting* and *emergency lighting*) shall be
emergency) provided and maintained on all parts of the *premises* to afford sufficient illumination to

allow the public and staff to move about safely and find their way to the exits at all times.

Battery 11 A *certificate* shall be submitted to the *Council* at least once every year in respect of the *emergency lighting* battery (including any self-contained units) and associated control equipment. The inspection of the battery and control equipment shall be in accordance with BS 5266-1. The *certificate* shall be signed by a Corporate Member of the Institution of Electrical Engineers or a member of the Electrical Contractors Association or by a contractor enrolled with the National Inspection Council for Electrical Installation Contracting or, with *consent*, another competent person.

Note: A competent person could, for example, be from a battery manufacturer.

Electrical 12 **(a)** A *certificate* shall be submitted to the *Council* at
installation least once every year in respect of the entire electrical installation (including the *emergency lighting* installation but excluding any battery.) The inspection shall be in accordance with Guidance Note 3 to BS 7671. In large or complex *premises* the electrical installation shall be visually inspected once a year and at least 20% of the installation tested in accordance with a programme approved by the *Council* such that the whole installation is tested every 5 years. The *certificate* shall be signed by a Corporate Member of the Institution of Electrical Engineers or a member of the Electrical Contractors Association or by a contractor currently enrolled with the National Inspection Council for Electrical Installation Contracting or, with *consent*, another competent person.

PART V
CONDITIONS RELATING TO THE SHOWING OF FILMS

Objection to the **13**
exhibition of a
film

If the Licensee is notified by the *Council* in writing that it objects to the exhibition of a film specifying the grounds of objection, such film shall not be exhibited.

Note: Any objection is likely to be on the ground that in the opinion of the *Council*:

(i) the film is likely

    (a) to encourage or incite to crime, or

    (b) to lead to disorder, or

    (c) to stir up hatred against any section of the public on grounds of colour, race or ethnic or national origin, disability, religious beliefs, sexual orientation or gender, or

    (d) to promote violence, sexual humiliation or degradation; or

(ii) the effect of the film is, if taken as a whole, such as to hold up to ridicule or contempt

    (a) people of a particular gender, sexual orientation, colour, race or ethnic or racial origin, or

    (b) people with disabilities or particular religious beliefs unless such film is depicting an historical event or should be exhibited in the public interest; or

(iii) the film contains a grossly indecent performance thereby outraging the standards of public decency.

Designation as **14**
unsuitable for
children

In respect of the categories 18 and RESTRICTED (18) as specified in Condition 15 where persons under the age of 16 are admitted to the *premises* the Licensee shall be responsible for designating films unsuitable for children and ensuring that such films are not exhibited to these persons.

ADDITIONAL CONDITIONS IN RESPECT OF FILMS EXHIBITED IN PUBLIC HOUSES

Film categories   **15**   **(a)**   The categories U, PG, 12A, 15 and 18 have the following meaning:

U   Universal – suitable for all.

PG   Parental Guidance. May be unsuitable for children under 8 years.

12A   May be unsuitable for children under 12 years. Children under 12 years must be accommpanied by an adult.

15   Suitable only for persons of 15 years and over.

18   Suitable only for adults.

RESTRICTED (18) Passed only for persons of 18 or over who are members (or their guests) of a properly constituted club.

(b)   The addition of the *Council*'s name (e.g. Guildford) after the category means that the film has been passed by the *Council* for exhibition in the *Council*'s area in the category shown.

Exhibition   **16**   No film shall be exhibited unless:
of films

(i)   it is a current news-reel; or

(ii)   it has been passed by the British Board of Film Classification and no notice of objection to its exhibition has been given by the *Council*;

or

(iii)   the film has been passed by the *Council*.

Restricted (18) 17 films – prohibition		Films in the RESTRICTED (18) category shall not be shown at the *premises*.

Unclassified films 18

Not less than 28 days' notice in writing shall be given to the *Council* of any proposal to exhibit any other film which has not been classified as specified in Condition 15. Such a film may only be exhibited if *consent* has been obtained and in accordance with the terms of any such *consent*.

Film categories 19 – Council's discretion

If the *Council* does not agree with the category of any film as passed by the British Board of Film Classification, it may alter the category or prohibit the showing of the film.

(a) On notice of alteration of category being given by the *Council* to the Licensee, the film shall thereafter be treated as being in the altered category and the Conditions applicable to the exhibition of films in the altered category shall be observed.

(b) On notice of prohibition of exhibition being given by the *Council* to the Licensee, the film shall not be exhibited.

Special Conditions 20

The Licensee shall comply with any Special Conditions that the *Council* may impose in respect of the exhibition of any film.

Films passed by 21 the Council – notice of exhibition

Before exhibiting a film not passed by the British Board of Film Classification but passed by the *Council*, or a film which has been passed by the Board but the category of which has been altered by the *Council*, the Licensee shall give notice to the *Council* of his intention to exhibit the film, specifying the name of the film and the dates on which the film is to be first exhibited and, except in the case of an emergency, such notice shall be given in writing at least 10 days before such date.

Category notices 22   **(a)**   Immediately before each exhibition at the *premises* of a film (other than a current news-reel) passed by the British Board of Film Classification there shall be exhibited on the screen for at least 10 seconds in such a manner as to be easily read by all persons in the auditorium a reproduction of the certificate of the Board or, as regards a *trailer*, of the statement approved by the Board indicating the category of the film.

   (b)   For a film passed by the *Council* notices shall be conspicuously displayed both inside and outside the *premises* so that persons entering can readily read them. The notices shall state without the addition of any other words:-

THE .... COUNCIL

(Here insert title of film) has been passed by the (insert name of *Council* concerned) as (here insert the definition of the category and the category assigned)

Where a *trailer* is to be exhibited advertising a film passed by the *Council* the notice shall state:-

THE .... COUNCIL
*........... trailer advertising +...... film
(*Here insert the category of the *trailer*)
(+Here insert the category of the film)

ANNEX 2

STANDARD CONDITIONS FOR EXHIBITION OF FILMS AND VIDEOS IN HOTELS

Standard Conditions in respect of premises licensed by ....Council for film exhibitions (including video) where such exhibitions are restricted to video exhibitions in hotel bedrooms or lounges where the exhibitions are incidental or subsidiary to the main use of the premises, in force from ....

These Conditions are divided into parts as follows:

INTRODUCTION

1. The Council may by way of Special Conditions dispense with or modify any Condition in any particular case. The Council may also impose additional Special Conditions in any particular case.

2. Any Licensee may apply to the Council in writing for any of the terms of the licence to be varied and, subject to any statutory enactment, if the Council so requires, the application must be advertised.

3. In order to reduce the length of this document, many Conditions rely upon the use of words precisely defined in Condition 1; such words are indicated by *italics*.

PART I
GENERAL

Definitions 1 In these Conditions the following words have the meanings indicated. Except where the context demands otherwise the singular includes the plural and the masculine includes the feminine. Words in *italics* throughout these Conditions denote words defined below.

Authorised Officer any police or fire officer or any person authorised in writing by the *Council*.

Consent permission given in advance by the *Council* in writing.

Council the licensing authority named on the licence.

Film exhibition any exhibition of moving pictures which is produced otherwise than by the simultaneous reception and exhibition of programmes included in a programme service within the meaning of the Broadcasting Act 1990.

Premises
all parts of the premises as licensed by the *Council* including the ancillary parts of the building such as offices, changing rooms, workshops, stores etc which are used in connection with the entertainment area.

Trailer
a film advertising a *film exhibition*.

PART II
RESPONSIBILITIES OF LICENSEE

Responsibility of Licensee   2   **(a)**   The Licensee shall, except with *consent*, retain control over all parts of the *premises*.

(b)   Either the Licensee or the Duty Manager shall be in charge of and within the *premises* whenever the *premises* are in use for the purposes of the licence. However the *Licensee* remains responsible for the observance of all licensing conditions.

(c)   The Licensee may authorise in writing a Duty Manager, who shall be at least 18 years old, to deputise for him. This written authorisation shall be kept on the *premises* and be readily available for examination by any *Authorised Officer*. The Licensee must be satisfied that anyone appointed as a Duty Manager understands the need to comply with the Conditions of the licence and is competent to perform the function of Duty Manager.

Note: Hereafter in these Conditions the term 'Licensee' will mean the Licensee or the Duty Manager as appropriate.

Staff 3 The Licensee shall ensure that he has sufficient trained staff on duty to ensure the safe evacuation of the *premises* in the event of emergency. Such staff shall have been specifically instructed on their duties in the event of an emergency by the Licensee or by a person nominated by him. The instruction given to staff shall include training on the safe and efficient running of the *premises* and the safe evacuation of the *premises*.

PART III
CONDITIONS RELATING TO THE SHOWING OF FILMS

Film categories 4 (a) The categories U, PG, 12A, 15 and 18 have the following meaning:

U   Universal – suitable for all.

PG   Parental Guidance. May be unsuitable for children under 8 years.

12A   May be unsuitable for children under 12 years. Children under 12 years must be accommpanied by an adult.

15   Suitable only for persons of 15 years and over.

18   Suitable only for adults.

RESTRICTED (18) Passed only for persons of 18 or over who are members (or their guests) of a properly constituted club.

(b) The addition of the *Council*'s name (e.g. Guildford) after the category means that the film has been passed by the *Council* for exhibition in the *Council*'s area in the category shown.

Exhibition 5 No film shall be exhibited unless:
of films
(i)   it is a current news-reel; or

(ii)   it has been passed by the British Board of Film Classification and no notice of objection to its

(iii)   exhibition has been given by the *Council*, or the film has been passed by the *Council*.

Restricted (18) 6
films - prohibition

Films in the RESTRICTED (18) category shall not be shown at the *premises*.

Unclassified films 7

Not less than 28 days' notice in writing shall be given to the *Council* of any proposal to exhibit any other film which has not been classified as specified in Condition 4. Such a film may only be exhibited if *consent* has been obtained and in accordance with the terms of any such *consent*.

Film categories - 8
Council's discretion

If the *Council* does not agree with the category of any film as passed by the British Board of Film Classification, it may alter the category or prohibit the showing of the film.

(a)   On notice of alteration of category being given by the *Council* to the Licensee, the film shall thereafter be treated as being in the altered category and the Conditions applicable to the exhibition of films in the altered category shall be observed.

(b)   On notice of prohibition of exhibition being given by the *Council* to the Licensee, the film shall not be exhibited.

Special 9
Conditions

The Licensee shall comply with any Special Conditions that the *Council* may impose in respect of the exhibition of any film.

Films passed 10
by the Council -
notice of exhibition

Before exhibiting a film not passed by the British Board of Film Classification but passed by the *Council*; or a film which has been passed by the Board but the category of which has been altered by the *Council*, the Licensee shall give notice to the *Council* of his intention to exhibit the film, specifying the name of the film and the dates on which the film is to be first exhibited and, except in the case of an emergency, such notice shall be given in writing at least 10 days before such date.

Category notices 11 **(a)** Immediately before each exhibition at the *premises* of a film (other than a current news-reel) passed by the British Board of Film Classification there shall be exhibited on the screen for at least 10 seconds in such a manner as to be easily read by all persons in the auditorium a reproduction of the certificate of the Board or, as regards a *trailer*, of the statement approved by the Board indicating the category of the film.

(b) For a film passed by the *Council* notices shall be conspicuously displayed both inside and outside the *premises* so that persons entering can readily read them. The notices shall state without the addition of any other words:-

THE .... COUNCIL
(Here insert title of film)
has been passed by the (insert name of
Council concerned) as
(here insert the definition of the category and
the category assigned)

Where a *trailer* is to be exhibited advertising a film passed by the *Council* the notice shall state:-

THE ....COUNCIL *.............
trailer advertising +...... film
(*Here insert the category of the _trailer_)
(+Here insert the category of the film)

Timetable of films   **12**   Guests shall be supplied with the details of the classification categories together with a timetable of films (with their categories indicated) to be shown.

Objection to the   **13**   If the Licensee is notified by the *Council* in
exhibition of a   writing that it objects to the exhibition of a film
film   specifying the grounds of objection, such film shall not be exhibited.

Note: Any objection is likely to be on the ground that in the opinion of the *Council*:

(i)   the film is likely

     (a)   to encourage or incite to crime, or

     (b)   to lead to disorder, or

     (c)   to stir up hatred against any section of the public on grounds of colour, race or ethnic or national origin, disability, religious beliefs, sexual orientation or gender, or

     (d)   to promote violence, sexual humiliation or degradation; or

(ii)   the effect of the film is, if taken as a whole, such as to hold up to ridicule or contempt

     (a)   people of a particular gender, sexual orientation, colour, race or ethnic or racial origin, or

     (b)   people with disabilities or particular religious beliefs unless such film is depicting an historical event or should be exhibited in the public interest; or

(iii)   the film contains a grossly indecent performance thereby outraging the standards of public decency.

This page is intentionally blank

ANNEX 3

STANDARD CONDITIONS WHEN PREMISES ARE USED OCCASIONALLY FOR PUBLIC ENTERTAINMENT

Foreword
These Conditions are standard licence conditions which must be observed whilst the premises are in use under the licence. They are, therefore, operational conditions.

In many cases the Council may require work to be done before a licence could be granted. Details of the likely technical requirements can be found in the Council's Technical Regulations. Alternatively applicants can discuss what is likely to be required with the Council's officers. Some of the Council's requirements will become licence conditions, for example, in most cases an accommodation limit will be put on the licence. In many cases the requirements when completed will become the approved arrangements which have to be maintained. (See Condition 13.)

In the case of outdoor events Council officers will wish to agree the detailed arrangements for the site with the applicant. Consequently as much notice as possible should be given of any outdoor event requiring an entertainments licence.

These Conditions are divided into parts as follows:

INTRODUCTION

1. The Council may by way of Special Conditions dispense with or modify any Condition in any particular case. The Council may also impose additional Special Conditions in any particular case.

2. Any Licensee may apply to the Council in writing for any of the terms of the licence to be varied and, subject to any statutory enactment, if the Council so requires, the application must be advertised.

3. In order to reduce the length of this document, many Conditions rely upon the use of words precisely defined in Condition 1; such words are indicated by *italics*.

PART I

GENERAL

Definitions   **1**   In these Conditions the following words have the meanings indicated. Except where the context demands otherwise the singular includes the plural and the masculine includes the feminine. Words in *italics* throughout these Conditions denote words defined below.

Approved   permitted in advance by the *Council* in writing.

Approved arrangements   the arrangement of the *premises*, (including the layout, fittings, installations and all other things in connection therewith) as *approved* by the *Council*.

Authorised Officer   any police or fire officer or any person authorised in writing by the *Council*.

Consent   permission given in advance by the *Council* in writing.

Council   the licensing authority named on the licence.

Emergency lighting   lighting provided for use in the event of the failure of the *normal lighting* system. Emergency lighting includes escape lighting.

Film exhibition   any exhibition of moving pictures which is produced otherwise than by the simultaneous reception and exhibition of programmes included in a programme service within the meaning of the Broadcasting Act 1990.

Normal lighting   all permanently installed electric lighting operating from the normal supply which, in the absence of adequate daylight, is intended for use during the whole time that the *premises* are occupied.

Note: Normal lighting does not include *emergency lighting*, purely decorative lighting and stage or performance lighting.

Premises all parts of the premises as licensed by the *Council* including the ancillary parts of the building such as offices, changing rooms, workshops, stores etc which are used in connection with the entertainment area.

Public persons, other than *staff* or performers, who are on the *premises*, whether or not they are members of a club and irrespective of payment.

Site any open air *premises*.

Staff any person, whether or not employed by the Licensee, concerned in the management, control or supervision of the *premises* who has been given specific responsibilities by the *Licensee* or person in charge.

Additional requirements 2 The Licensee or his representative shall comply with any additional requirements found to be necessary by the *Council's* officers during or after inspection of the arrangements or during the event.

Hours 3 The *premises* shall not open to the *public* before 9.00 a.m. or be kept open beyond 11.00 p.m. (midnight for plays and *film exhibitions*) unless otherwise specified on the licence.

PART II
PARTICULAR RESPONSIBILITIES OF LICENSEE

Person in charge of premises 4 **(a)** The Licensee shall retain control over all parts of the *premises*.

(b) Either the Licensee or some responsible person nominated by him in writing for the purpose shall be in charge of and within the *premises* whenever the *public* are present. However the *Licensee* remains responsible for the observance of all licensing conditions.

Staff 5 **(a)** The Licensee shall ensure that he has sufficient trained *staff* on duty to ensure the safe evacuation of the *premises* in the event of emergency. Such *staff* shall be familiar with the layout of the *premises* and have been specifically instructed on their duties in the event of an emergency by the Licensee or by a person nominated by him. The instruction given to *staff* shall include training on the safe and efficient running of the *premises* and the safe evacuation of the *premises*.

(b) All attendants or stewards shall be clearly identifiable and in position prior to the admission of the *public* onto the *premises*.

Overcrowding 6 The Licensee shall ensure that the accommodation limit(s) specified on the licence are not exceeded and shall be aware of the number of the *public* on the *premises*. This information shall immediately be provided on request to any *Authorised Officer*.

Special risks	7	The Licensee shall not permit an entertainment that involves special risks except with *consent*. The Licensee shall inform the *Council* of any proposed demonstrations/displays involving the use of animals, motor cycles, vehicles, explosives and of any other proposals which may involve a special risk.
Special effects	8	The Licensee shall not permit the use of special effects, except with *consent*. Special effects include the use of dry ice machines, cryogenic fogs, smoke machines, fog generators, pyrotechnics and fireworks, real flame, firearms, motor vehicles, strobe lighting and lasers.
Prevention of nuisance	9	The *Licensee* shall ensure that no nuisance is caused by noise emanating from the *premises* or by vibration transmitted through the structure of the *premises*.
Hypnotism	10	No performance of hypnotism (as defined in the Hypnotism Act 1952) shall take place.

PART III
SANITARY ARRANGEMENTS

Toilet facilities	11	Toilet facilities as specified by the *Council* shall be provided free of charge and be kept clean and in proper working order.
Drinking water	12	Where free drinking water is provided for the *public*, it shall, except with *consent*, only be provided in a supervised area. Drinking water taps shall be clearly marked as such.

PART IV
CONDITIONS RELATING TO SAFETY INCLUDING FIRE SAFETY

Approved   **13**   **(a)**   No alterations shall be made to the *approved*
arrangements   *arrangements* including the layout, fittings, facilities and fire-fighting equipment, except with *consent.* The *approved arrangements* shall be maintained in good condition and full working order.

           (b)   Adequate fire-fighting equipment shall be provided. The equipment shall have been tested within the last 12 months and have the date of test clearly indicated on the appliance.

           (c)   The *public* shall not be admitted to the *premises* until all the *Council*'s requirements have been met, including the testing of any gas and electrical installations and the submission of any certificates required by the *Council.*

Escape routes   **14**   **(a)**   All escape routes and exits including external exits shall be maintained unobstructed, in good order with non-slippery and even surfaces, free of trip hazards and clearly identified.
           Note: In *premises* where chairs and tables are provided care should be taken that clear gangways are maintained.

           (b)   All exit doors shall be available and easily openable without the use of a key, card, code or similar means. Only *approved* fastenings shall be used.

           (c)   Any removable security fastenings shall be removed from the doors prior to opening the *premises* to the *public.* All such fastenings shall be kept in the *approved* position(s).

(d) If *required*, exit doors shall be secured in the fully open position when the *public* are present.

(e) All fire doors shall be maintained effectively self-closing and shall not be held open other than by *approved* devices.

(f) Fire-resisting doors to ducts, service shafts and cupboards shall be kept locked shut.

(g) The edges of the treads of steps and stairways shall be maintained so as to be conspicuous.

Curtains, decorations etc.   **15**

(a) Hangings, curtains and temporary decorations shall not be used without *consent*.

Note: The *Council* will normally require any hangings, curtains and temporary decorations to be maintained flame-retarded.

(b) Hangings, curtains and temporary decorations shall be so arranged so as not to obstruct fire safety signs or fire-fighting equipment.

Lighting (normal and emergency)   **16**

Two independent systems of lighting (*normal lighting* and *emergency lighting*) shall be provided and maintained on all parts of the *premises* to afford sufficient illumination to allow the *public* and *staff* to move about safely and find their way to the exits at all times.

Heating appliances   **17**

Portable heating or cooking appliances shall not be used within a building without *consent*.

Outbreaks of fire   **18**

The fire brigade shall be called at once to any outbreak or suspected outbreak of fire, however slight. Notices detailing the actions to be taken in the event of fire or other emergencies, including how the fire brigade can be summoned, shall be prominently displayed and shall be protected from damage or deterioration.

Disabled people 19 The Licensee shall ensure that, whenever disabled people are present, adequate arrangements are made to enable their safe evacuation in the event of an emergency and that they are made aware of these arrangements.

Note: Licensees are advised to obtain details of and seek to address any special needs when approached by organisers of parties of disabled people.

PART V
ADDITIONAL CONDITIONS APPLICABLE TO OUTDOOR EVENTS, FILM EXHIBITIONS AND INDOOR SPORTS

A. OUTDOOR EVENTS

INTRODUCTION

The *Council* will normally expect compliance with the relevant recommendations of the *Events Safety Guide* published by the Health and Safety Executive. For larger scale events, such as pop concerts, the *Council* may make many more detailed and specific requirements than are contained in these standard conditions. The *Events Safety Guide* provides guidance for the promoters of such events.

Completion 20 No members of the *public* shall be admitted to the *site* until all construction has been completed and contractors equipment and vehicles have been removed from the *site* or placed in a compound.

Site layout	**21**		The *approved* layout of the *site*, including the positioning of all stalls and concessions shall not be altered without *consent.*
Rubbish	**22**		Provision shall be made for the safe storage of all rubbish including that generated from the concessionaires. Litter bins on the *site* shall be emptied at regular intervals.
Vehicles	**23**	**(a)**	No vehicles shall be allowed to enter or move around the *site* while the *site* is open to the *public* (except for emergency vehicles attending an incident or essential site service or other *approved* vehicles.)
		(b)	Access to the *site* for emergency vehicles shall be maintained clear of obstructions at all times.
Contact point	**24**		The Licensee shall establish a contact point, which shall be permanently *staffed* during the whole time the *site* is open to the *public*. The contact point shall be provided with a telephone and instructions for contacting the emergency services.
Noise control	**25**		Any noise limits imposed on the Licensee by the *Council* shall not be exceeded. The Licensee shall provide the *Council* with a contact telephone number, effective during the event, where direct contact can be made in the event of noise complaints being received.
Lost children	**26**		Suitable provision shall be made for lost children.

B. FILM EXHIBITIONS

**Compliance with 27
Standard Conditions**

The Licensee shall comply with the *Council's* Additional Conditions A and C for *premises* used as cinemas (copies attached as applicable.)

Safety film 28

Only safety film shall be brought on to the *premises*.

**Screen and 29
masking**

The picture screen and any temporary proscenium or masking, curtains, draperies, or decorations, shall be non-combustible or maintained flame-retarded to the *Council's* satisfaction.

**Projection 30
apparatus**

Any projection apparatus shall be installed in an *approved* position and shall be surrounded by an *approved* barrier.

C. INDOOR SPORTS

**Compliance with 31
Standard Conditions**

The Licensee shall comply with the *Council's* Additional Conditions SE for premises used for indoor sports entertainment (copy attached if applicable.)